How I Learned to Love You

Skadi Cooke

For permission requests, please contact publishing.vultureandcrone@gmail.com or visit us at www.vultureandcrone.com

Note: for privacy reasons, names, locations, and dates may have been changed.

Book Cover and Photography by Skadi Cooke

First printing edition 2023

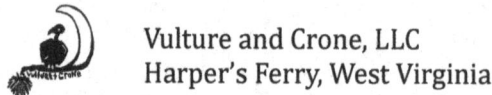

Vulture and Crone, LLC
Harper's Ferry, West Virginia

ISBN : 979-8-9886063-2-1

for my gorgeous boy

4

Table of Contents

Acknowledgements

To Tim: thank you for the mundane things, like checking for typos and changing diapers. Thank you for the miraculous things, like helping me find my way back to our family every time I get lost. Thank you for loving me, always and every day, unconditionally. You are my safe space, and I am forever grateful.

To Grandma: thank you for being my first child and my surrogate mom. You taught me to be stubborn and brave and to live life with an obstinate sort of joy. I miss you every fucking day because you loved me hard.

To Elise: thank you for pushing me, holding my hand, and always reminding me that I am doing my best.

To Kat: you get my weird, dude. I love you.

To Biz, Theresa (and really everyone at One Bad Mother): finding your show was my first step out of the forest. You helped me actually believe I'd find my way out. Thank you. You are all doing such a fucking good job.

Thank you to Bex, Brigitte, and Meagan for reading my shitty first draft, and to Coll for never getting irritated when I bounced graphic designs off of you. You all gave me the confidence to keep going.

Thank you to all of my chosen family for loving me when I feel unlovable and for accepting every part of who I am. Thank you for being our village and helping us raise this child.

To Mom, Dad, and the rest: "... here is my thanks to the monster who didn't succeed in swallowing me alive."
- Nietzsche

Content Warnings

This work discusses depression, postpartum depression/psychosis, suicidal ideation, self-harm ideation, disordered eating, abuse (emotional, financial, emotional incest), and narcissism.

I also use the word "fuck" quite liberally.

Prologue

Few will admit it, but not all parents start out loving their children. And, while some learn how along the way, there are those who never do.

It took me eleven months and a handful of days before I loved you, my gorgeous boy. This is our story.

One

When I was fifteen, I lost my mind. An adolescent brain can only handle so much apathy, and I was drowning in it. Literally.

Night after night, I dreamt of falling into a thick, wet abyss. I'd wake up covered in sweat and piss, then change the sheets and turn on all the lights. I'd curl around a stuffed animal - yours now - and beg the universe to send someone who could hold me and tell me it would be okay.

No one came, though.

Of course, I never expected them to, either.

My parents divorced when I was three or so, and while I saw Dad often enough, I lived with Mom. All my friends loved her. My mom was the cool one; everyone knew her asher as the funny one who always let me go out and gossiped with my friends about their growing boobs oror hot boys. "She's so chill," they'd say, jealous. No one knew the rest, though: that she routinely stayed in bed, or in a tattered robe, until noon for most of my childhood. No one knew she wouldn't talk to me for days. No one knew how she'd stare, empty, while my step dad yelled at me and my brothers.

Now I understand that empty stare. It's called dissociating. I do it, too.

the strange and familiar

when I was a child, I lost
myself to noface shadows and
black water. I knew this -
mothering -
would be ...
magical and terrible and too filled with
otherness for words, but
   I never thought
   I'd be choking up
   water again.

When I held you on my chest, a few minutes
after they pulled you from my stomach, my mind
pulled away from my body. I remember looking
in at myself through the doorway, and I am still
haunted by the look on my own face. You were
perfect: strong and solid. In a lifetime of
hallucinations, you were the truest thing I'd ever
seen. Yet, I couldn't believe it. Believe you. I
couldn't believe you were mine. I was filled with
so much unbelieving that my face contorted into
the broken kind of grief of a woman who had
forgotten how to scream.

after

I woke up soft:
opened, closed, and missing
my son.

"Wanna hold him, mama?"

hands offer
a small boy with quiet eyes
that remind me of someone.
but I'm no one's mama anymore.
I am an ocean of blood.
"No."

Two

A few months before my sixteenth birthday, I went with friends to see *The Exorcist*. I remember seeing the words "help me" written across that little girl's abdomen, and I felt eerily seen. Before that, sometimes, when I was alone in the house, I would wonder if Mom would pay attention to my pain if I just bled a little. I didn't want to kill myself, but I couldn't stop wondering; if I opened up a vein, just a little, would she finally help me? If I dug into my stomach, just a little, would she listen when the doctors told her I was unwell? And now, here was this girl, nearly my own age, begging for the same thing on the screen: help me, mommy... help me.

That was the first time I hallucinated. From the corners of the movie theater, dark figures, tall and slender, watched me. Shadowmen. Their hands, with thin and spindly fingers, unfurled towards me, inviting me into the dark. I didn't tell anybody. I had brothers to take care of and tests to ace and exercise to do and a job to find. I was a good girl, and good girls didn't hallucinate.

I spent the night at a friend's and hoped to wake up normal - back to my old self - but I did not. The Shadowmen followed me from her house, to the school bus, to the school, and back to my own home. When I walked in the door, Mom took a look at my face and erupted into giggles; "I told you it was going to be too scary for you," she teased.

"I'm fine," I grumbled. I headed towards my room, and the Shadowmen followed me downstairs.

I lasted five more days.

I don't remember this, but on the sixth day, on a Thursday morning, I called my Dad and whispered "I can't go to school, and I can't stay home. I'm not safe here." Truthfully, I wasn't really safe with Dad, either, but I didn't know that back then. That part comes later.

Dad picked me up, and I spent the day wandering around the outside of his job's campus. I stood in the middle of a small field, with grass as far as the sun would let me see. Her heat on my face felt like two gentle hands holding me. I closed my eyes and turned my face towards her, letting a warm, red glaze fill the space behind my eyelids. When I finally pulled my face away and opened my eyes, all I saw was grass and sky and a few people walking their dogs. The Shadowmen were gone.

When I went back into the building to find Dad, they were waiting for me. But they were smaller now, less imposing, and the screaming in my head - my own thoughts scared that I was going crazy, I was going crazy, I was going crazy - was down to a quiet din.

By the end of the day, I knew enough to know I wouldn't survive if it all came blaring back, but I was terrified of being locked away somewhere, and I was ashamed. *If you hadn't insisted on*

watching that stupid movie, I thought to myself,
*you wouldn't even be in this mess. Mom was right.
She told you it was too scary and she was fucking
right, idiot.*

So I didn't tell Dad the whole truth. Instead, in
the car on the way back to his apartment, I told
him, "I don't think I can go home. I think... I
think I need to stay with you for a little longer."

I expected a lot of questions, but he didn't ask
a single one. He nodded, drove silently for a few
minutes, then told me one of us was going to
have to talk to Mom. "I need to do it," I said.

Two days later, I was in a burger shop trying
to explain to her that I was terrified and broken,
and I needed to stay somewhere where I wasn't
going to drown in my own bed. "I'm so sorry," I
offered. "But I can't go back right now."

Just like with Dad, though, I stopped short of
the whole truth. I didn't tell her I was seeing
things. I didn't tell her I had to fight an urge to
bleed every time I walked into the kitchen. I
didn't tell her I was pretty sure Death was
waiting for me back in my bedroom. Maybe if I
had, she would have reacted differently. I'll never
know.

As it was, she offered me the same cool,
menacing expression she reserved for
incompetent retail clerks. "You can come home
tomorrow or you're not welcome at all," she told
me. "I will not have you going back and forth and
jerking me around." I watched her perfectly

manicured candy red nail circle around the top of the styrofoam cup. "I do not deserve that."

Everything I refused to say aloud to her raged in my own head: *But I'm dying. Please. Just look. I'm so hurt and small and scared and please just… please.*

I didn't say it, though. I couldn't. Something in her eyes warned me it wasn't safe. I wasn't safe. So, I did my best to match her unimpressed gaze. "Okay," I said. "I'll get my things after school next week." Then, somehow, I stood up and left her behind.

As Dad drove back to his apartment, I sobbed the sort of crying that comes out like screams and rips your bones. It felt as if my tears gathered at my feet, the water rising to my waist, my chest, my neck. By the time we got back to the apartment, I felt as if I was permanently near-drowning in a tank of murky water. There was just a little bit of space at the top - just enough so that if I pushed off the bottom in exactly the right way, I could gasp and almost breathe.

I lived that way for two years. That's how long it took to remember I could break the glass and find my own peace.

***

If a woman has experienced depression before, her odds of experiencing postpartum depression rise significantly. They rise higher if she has an anxiety disorder, and higher still if she has a family history of any of the above. So, when you were born, I was prepared for the water to rise up around my knees again. But, by this point - a full twenty years after that day in the burger shop - I thought I was ready. I took medication. I had a therapist. I had a meticulous self care strategy for those first ninety days. And, I was going to advocate for myself in the hospital.

I was ready.

The only problem was that you, little sir, were not.

Truly, you seemed to have no interest in being born whatsoever.

I tried to tell them - doctors, midwives - but they all said you were late. As if my body was a station waiting for a train. They spun horror stories about your heart rate and fingernails. So, even though I knew - every part of my body knew - that you needed a few more days, I did what I was supposed to. I listened to the doctors. I went to the hospital. At every intervention, I said yes.

cervix softener

"discomfort," they tell me, "is common."
I sit, icepack between
my thighs, and force a smile
when they spread me wide:
an intern cannot mask her horror; "her insides
are like ground meat."
the midwife is visibly irked

I'm only at three inches.

a day and an inch later

I don't want anyone's fingers
inside me anymore.

we beg

for them to cut me open.
Pitocin is safer, they say.
"think of the baby."

"She's not progressing"

I feel you
- inside me and terrified -
swim under my ribs. They say
your heart is fine,
but I
know better:
we are not safe here.

epidural

I think I hear me screaming.
        please, jesus, make me a stone.
a trio of nurses holds me
down.

cold
pours in.

I pushed for four hours.
It was nothing like the movies. The midwife
kept putting her fingers in my ass. The intern
kept trying to hold my hand. And your daddy -
who I needed so badly to kiss my forehead and
tell me it would all be over soon, was forced to
hold up a dead weight leg instead.
Eventually, the surgeon popped in, all clean
shaven and smiles, to tell me they would cut you
out instead.
At that point, days without sleep had rendered
me incapable of hiding my panic. The idea of
surgery - of hands inside me - of being
unconscious or worse when you were born... it
all spilled out of me in the form of shaking limbs
and gasping breaths.
But he didn't seem to notice. No one did.

c-section

the surgical lights are still off.
reflective lenses of a stainless steel fly.
I'm forced to
to see what they see:
    a naked girl.
    walleyed.
    inside her
    screwed tight mouth

is screaming.
a blue curtain goes up, lights blare on,
and I close my body down.
I try not to listen
as they make a meal of me.

They tell me you came out with a sturdy grip
and eyes wide open. I don't remember any of
that. I only remember darkness and laughter.
  But, I did wake up. As you fell asleep on me, I
did. And even though I was still numb and
emptier than I had ever been, the water only
sloshed around my neck, and I had hope - real
hope - that as my body unnumbed, my brain
would too, and maybe I could love you.
  Then you woke up. Hungry.

cluster

every hour (going on thirty something now),
you scream to feed.
  we call the night nurses,
  but "it's normal."
  we ask for the lactation consultant,
  but "it's night."
  we ask for a break
  but "the nursery is full."
  finally, your daddy
  finds formula.
  you drink two bottles in twenty minutes.
  It's the first time I fail you.

Failure.
Failure.
Failure.
The word echoed in my head like a heartbeat.
By the time you had finished your second bottle,
I was drowning again.

Three

Long before I knew I wanted to be a mother, I was raised to take care. It's ironic; both Mom and Dad presented as being sexually progressive - Mom with her short hair and unshaven legs, Dad with his open talk of the importance of female orgasm - but really, they raised me to be as traditional as they came.

Mom had an in-house daycare, and I had two younger brothers. During the school year, I'd help everyone get their bags together and help the babies get settled after they'd been dropped off in the mornings. During the summer, I fixed scrapes and painted nails, made snacks and chaperoned walks, and - maybe most importantly - I was the in-house therapist. Whenever anyone fought or had a problem, it was my job to help settle them down.

I don't remember Mom ever explicitly explaining this to me. It's just how it was.

My bed became a sanctuary for other children. "Johnny is driving me crazy," a little girl would complain, "can I sit in here with you?" Or "Tracy just told me I cant play with the other girls. I hate her," another would say, crying. "And I think I like a boy at school. What do I do?"

A few years into this, I turned 12, and that meant I was legally allowed to stay home and watch the kids. So, that summer, Mom started leaving us alone. She'd run to the bank, or the Wawa. Never more than an hour away. Just long enough for me to change a diaper or two, yell "stop it," a couple times and clean a stain out of something.

I loved it, though. I loved the importance of it. All my friends were playing with dolls or toys and here I was with a live, squirming infant in my arms and a couple toddlers at my feet. Their mothers all doted on me at pick up; "god, she's so responsible," "I hope my daughter is as sweet as you," "you are just the perfect little mother, aren't you?"

It wasn't long before I started babysitting outside the house. By the time I was fourteen, I was working most weekends and had a few regular families. They were good people; food was always in the fridge, there was always a blanket for me to curl up in, and their kids were the kind of carefree you see on television.

I was safe in those houses.

***

As I sat in the hospital bed after you were born, feeling held together by prayer and gauze, I remembered how it felt to curl up on another person's couch and listen to the delicious silence that is born of safety. Not because I felt safe - I absolutely did not – but because I knew that you were. Even as I was terrified - of the increasing pain, of the wires that led from me to god knows where, of the fact that I needed help to do entirely anything - I knew that you were bathed in safety. And, thanks to your daddy, you were loved.

birth day

I watch my partner (my heart,
my anchor, and the rest) stand over the
plexiglass bassinet
and smile.
It hurts
in a way I don't understand and don't want to.
So,
I decide -
your daddy will love you. and I...
I will keep you safe.

Four

I don't remember the moment when I realized I was unsafe in my own home. But, I do remember that I met my stepdad when I was six, and I knew he was an asshole from the start: the kind of guy who'd squash a beetle just to watch it writhe.

I remember watching him meet my little brother, Josh, for the first time. He had an awkward gait; everything was exaggerated, goofy. He was clearly trying to make Josh, then three, laugh. Then, he was down on the floor with my brother, "wrasslin'," as he called it. But I didn't like the way his big hands wrapped around my brother's legs. I didn't like the way he pushed Josh a little too fiercely into the floor. I didn't like the way he tickled - past the point of giggles and into breathlessness. I started walking towards them, but Mom stopped me. "Girls. don't. wrestle."

A few months later, after we were all living together, I grabbed the cordless phone and hid in my room. "Daddy? Daddy. He hit him. He hit him on the butt, daddy and now Josh isn't allowed to come out of his room."

Dad was a force back then, and through the phone I could hear the roar in the back of his throat as he told me to stay in my room and wait. He drove immediately over. Forty minutes later, I heard a knock on the door and then his voice flooded the foyer. "I am his father. Me. And if that piece of shit touches my son again I will -"

He didn't get to say what, though, because Mom was pleading over him. She was crying and screaming, standing halfway down the steps, blocking her husband, who stood silently behind her, glaring. I watched my father carefully, and took his rage as permission: it was okay to hate this guy. So, I did. It felt good, coiled and hot, in the bottom of my core.

Not long after this, Josh and I were with Dad in a garden center. It was around the holidays, and Josh wandered off after someone in a Rudolph suit wielding candy. I remember the terror on Dad's face at realizing his son was lost, and I remember the calm determination when we got home and he told Josh to take off his pants and lay across Dad's knee.

I watched the first spank, and I watched Josh cry. I listened to Dad calmly explain how he had to do this, so Josh would know never to get lost again.

As I write this now, my gut churns the way it did then. Even now, after all these thirty-some years, I still don't understand how a parent could so calmly traumatize their child. I don't understand why he thought biological fatherdom made it ok. Why could he hit Josh, but not my stepdad? I still want to ask him - Is it because it makes the child your property somehow? Yours to do with as you choose? Even if I agreed, I still

don't understand: why would you want to break
your things?

I watched two more smacks. Then, he helped
Josh up and told him he could go play. My toddler
brother wiped his eyes and left the room. I did
not. I folded my arms and stared down at my
father with all of the fury I had. He saw me, and
he gave me the same rationalization he had told
Josh, but I was unimpressed. Something had
rooted me to the ground and I was terrified - of
it, of my dad, of everything. I couldn't speak.
Eventually, Dad stopped trying and left the room,
and I went to check on Josh. He seemed fine
enough, but I was not. I couldn't bring myself to
talk to Dad for the rest of the weekend.

After he drove us back to Mom's, he held me
back while my baby brother went ahead. "I'm
sorry," he said. His voice was small and
confusing.

I responded fast. "Never again."

He nodded and repeated. "Never."

***

As far as I know, Dad didn't hit Josh again until
Josh was old enough to hit back. Neither did my
stepdad. But there was another baby to worry
about: Will.

When I was seven, Mom and my stepdad had
Will. He was this delicious hunk of fat and smiles,
and I was completely in love with him. I knew
every freckle, every strand of hair. I even loved
his ridiculous lopsided cone head that stuck

around long after his birth. Whereas Josh was my partner in crime, Will was my baby in training.

It was routine for my stepdad to come home for lunch, and on this particular day he was upstairs with Will while Mom and I were downstairs with some of the daycare kids. I still remember the sound: a thwack followed by a child's scream. It was one of those loud wailing sounds that screws itself right into your bones. It was Will.

He scrambled down the stairs on his shaking toddler legs. Mom was sitting next to me, fixing a girl's hair. We looked at one another and called out to him, "what's wrong baby? What happened?"

He couldn't say. He could barely breathe. He fell down the last step and tumbled forward into my lap. He wrapped his arms around my legs and sobbed. His whole body shook as I hoisted him into my lap.

Mom watched him carefully. She was so weirdly calm. Quietly, she pointed at a red mark that poked out from above his diaper. Gingerly, she pulled his diaper away from his skin and revealed a painful-looking, swollen handprint. It was as if someone had colored with a marker on his skin.

I looked over to her and we stared into each other's eyes. "It's going to be okay," she whispered. "You tell him it's going to be okay."

I held him tight and watched her walk, slow and measured, upstairs. A door opened, then slammed shut. Then, there was screaming. My mother does not raise her voice. Ever. But that day, even the neighbors heard.

Some minutes later, my stepdad came down the stairs with her. Like my father that day in the car, he was smaller now. Weak. Behind him, Mom was taller than I'd ever seen her. I didn't know it at the time, but Mom was intimately acquainted with violence. Her dad hit her, and mine was the kind of guy who broke plates and let her imagine the marks instead. But now, she looked like steel. I caught her eye and silently agreed to the vow; no one would hurt our boys again.

A couple years later, when I was eleven, I saw a neighborhood boy, Simon, slap Josh. I had no idea what preceded the slap, and I didn't care. I dropped my bike to the ground, rushed to his yard and grabbed Simon's hand so hard I nearly dislocated his shoulder. I dragged him, screaming, into our yard, and tossed him to the ground like the trash I'd decided he was. Then I kicked. Again and again.

My stepdad had to pull me off. "You are grounded young lady!" He tried to push me into the house, but I shoved back and walked deliberately up the concrete stairs. I only turned around long enough to watch Simon stagger up to his feet and shuffle away before I opened the front door, went to my room, and waited for someone to come yell at me.

After a few hours, though, it was clear no one was coming to enforce the grounding. That night, at dinner, no one even mentioned it. But I noticed Mom had made my favorite meal, and I got an extra helping of ice cream for dessert. She even let me stay up an hour late to watch television.

Five

We brought you home on a Tuesday. It's wild if you think about it. On the last Tuesday in May, you were a concept floating around inside me. On the first Tuesday in June, you were a life.

"just drive"

the aide rolls us out into the sun
and you are, amusingly, unimpressed.
your daddy waits at the car with a smile
that rivals the sky.
the aide lets go,
and I wonder if one day
I'll forget her chipping purple nails and faded
ombre hair or the fact that she was going home
to cook mac n cheese for her boyfriend and was
starting nursing school in the fall...

I hope so.

The hospital was within walking distance of our apartment, but the drive somehow took years. We stopped at every light, and each time I fought the urge to turn around and check; were you still breathing?

When we were finally home, we walked into our apartment building, originally a retirement center, and the hallway smelled like grandparents. Specifically, that day, it smelled like Grandma: old perfume, musty clothes and bargain brand cleaner. Your daddy held you carefully, like a secret, close to his chest, and I felt the smell follow us into our home. Grandma had been dead for two years at this point, but I swear her papery fingers settled softly onto my shoulder.

It was the same apartment, same room, same everything as just a week before. Everything was the same except for me. I was empty and missing. For the first time, I was almost happy Grandma was dead. I doubted she'd have recognized me anymore.

homecoming

for days I'd prayed
to see my dogs, and now here they are
eyeing me careful: stranger.
the truth of it kills.
I leave. sit on the toilet. bleed.
the eldest follows
slowly. his nose
takes him to between my thighs, and
I watch him breathe.
he looks up. whimpers. Then,
before I can lie (it's ok)
he's in my arms and licking me - the tears

don't even have a chance to fall - I
grab tight / breathe in / laugh soft
(he always smells like summer)
 and wonder if maybe - just maybe - I'm still
me.

The next two weeks were like living inside a
Picasso: beautiful and meaningful from the
outside, but just a fucking mess firsthand. In an
ideal world, I would have had a mom or an
auntie, a grandmother - someone - to remind me
to eat and to help you sleep and to promise that
it's not always going to hurt this bad when I
shower. But I didn't have anyone like that. I just
had your daddy. And your daddy was
wonderful... but it was not the same.

Still, even though I wasn't entirely convinced I
could keep the both of us alive, I was determined
to breastfeed. I might not have had actual women
folk to tell me it was the best thing to do, but it
was in all the books, on all the hospital walls, in
all the podcasts and blogs: breast is best. So, I
forced myself to find the will to eat instead of
doing what I actually wanted to. I wanted to
crawl under the bed, and dig a hole through the
carpet, concrete , and foundation. I wanted to be
alone and cold in the dirt. I sure as hell did not
want to pump. But, I forced myself to do that, too.
After that night in the hospital, I needed to know
you were getting enough to eat. I needed to see
the mililiters for myself.

moo

I am
simultaneously
entranced and repulsed
by pumping.

I doubt I'll ever eat beef again.

About a week in, I found myself sitting on the couch, half watching the television, pumping, and eating cold chili directly from the can with a spork. I saw myself from above, and it was a darkly hilarious sight. Stereotypical in its awfulness. I set the can down and reached for my phone to text someone, but couldn't think of anyone who would understand.

white lies

I'm so happy.
He's perfect.
We're doing fine.

The only place anything made sense was outside in the sun. It seemed like she was the only thing in my entire universe that remained unchanged. I pushed my broken body outside to see her every day, even if I could only manage to stand for a few minutes.

She

pours herself over me
until my bones
are warm,
soft,
listening to the quiet all around me.
a few neighbors see me
(doubled over, crying)
as I walk. I smile
before they can ask if
I'm ok.

I kept staring into your face, hoping to see my
son, but every time I searched your comically fat
cheeks, I saw a stranger. You just looked like a
baby. Any baby. Cute enough, sure, but not
particularly special. I felt like I had all those years
ago as a babysitter; I was just waiting for my shift
to end and your momma to come and take you
home. I was just keeping you safe in the
meantime.

help

they say baby blues
are normal,
but, I think -
there are faces in the shadows and whispers in
the shower and I have to work so hard not to claw

*my hands into my own skin... even when boychild
is sleeping and sweetness and light... I can't sleep.
Please don't make me sleep.*
  - maybe something's wrong.

     It wasn't just that I didn't think that you
were mine. The truth was, most days, I didn't
even want you to be. I was desperate for your
mother to come back, to relieve me, to let me
slink off to the nearest shower and fall asleep
until I drowned. I couldn't bear the idea that it
was just me: that no one was coming. I must have
said once a day for months that I'd wished we'd
just gotten a third dog. I knew who I would be
with three dogs. I knew what that life would look
like. But with you... the future was locked away
behind a wall of black glass.
     Looking back, though, I think there was more.
I think I was terrified to lose you. Maybe more
scared than I had ever been of everything.
Because I had lost a child before. Not a
miscarriage, or even an actual human child. (And
please don't think I'm trying to minimize the pain
of mothers who've outlived their loves.) But, to
an unwanted fourteen year old girl, a two pound
four week old kitten feels like a child. She felt like
love, and she'd been mine for just under a week.
     My friends had bought her for my birthday,
and I was immediately besotted. She was small
enough to snuggle in the palm of my hand; she
could have been a pile of dryer lint curled on my
pillow. When her eyes - perfectly round and

electric blue - were closed, she nearly disappeared. So, we named her Zero.

Mom was irritated when I showed her my new joy, but she told me I could keep her as long as she stayed in my room until we knew she was litter trained. I agreed. That night, she slept on my chest, so small I barely registered her heartbeat. In the morning, I checked for anything that might hurt her, left some toys on the bed and some food in the corner, and I carefully closed the door as tight as it would go.

But, somehow, she got out. And it kept happening.

The first day, I found her running from the dog, scooped up her trembling body and held her close against my face. I cooed at her until she fell asleep in my lap in the safety of our room.

The next day, I found her cowering under my bed. "She got out, but I caught her," Mom told me, her voice flat.

On the third day, Mom opened my door wide, and the dog came barreling in. Zero tried to run up Mom's leg, but Mom hissed at her. I opened my mouth to object and rushed to pick my baby up.

Mom chuckled. "If only you'd take such good care of your dishes," she said. She motioned with a disdainful wave to an empty cereal bowl from the night before. She shooed out the dog and flopped down onto the bed. "I know you like this little thing," she said, "but your stepdad's allergies have started acting up again. It can't stay here. Maybe your father will take it."

At first, it seemed like a reasonable alternative. After all, Dad loved cats. He'd had a series of them over the years. So, I was cautiously optimistic. I took Zero with me to his apartment and pleaded for her to stay. "Come on, sweetie," he said. "You know I work crazy hours. And you're only here on the weekends anyway. I can't take care of it the rest of the time."

I wanted to tell him that she was my heart - that I'd never felt my own heart before, but here it was in front of me, all small and scared, and I needed him to please - please help me keep her safe. I stood in front of him, imagining it all in my head: I'd get on my knees, I'd cry and plead. But even in my imagination, his jaw stayed set and his eyes stayed narrowed and he still said firmly: no.

That evening, I called a friend of a friend. She was sweet enough; her parents had a good chunk of land and dozens of cats, and she was all too happy to have one more. I told Dad after I'd made the call, and he told me he was proud of how I'd "taken care of it."

The following day, when I got back to Mom's, my stepfather drove me to give my baby away. I held her close to me the whole time. We were in his stupid convertible with the top down, and she still fell asleep curled in my hands, cupped against my chest.

You'll be safe now. I thought it over and over as loud as I could. *And I will forever remember.*

I dropped her off, then stayed silent for the drive home. I refused to cry or scream. He tried to get me talking about whatever was on the radio, but I refused that, too. I knew I was making him uncomfortable, and that was, at least, something. He continued babbling on as we got home, then he followed me down into my room. "You did the right thing," he said, echoing Dad. I took a step back, and he ignored my body language. Instead, he forced a hug onto me and pressed my head into his chest. He smelled like menthols and sweat, and I wondered how long I'd have to wait before the cigarettes killed him.

I kept my arms at my side and waited for him to be done with me. He finally let go of my shoulders and backed away towards the door, meeting my empty expression with an awkward smile. Mom was now in the hallway, calling to him. She took his hand, then she told me it was nearly time for dinner.

Six

The year beforeI left Mom's, and shortly after losing Zero, I started walking outside. I wasn't going any place in particular. I just needed to... leave. I'd come home from school and my stepdad would be there, sitting on the family computer, right outside my room, filling the hallway with cigarette smoke and hostility. Some days, I'd say hello and get ignored. Other days, I'd stay quiet and get a "what, you can't even bother with a hello? You know, I pay for that door you're about to walk through. You'd better not slam it, either."

It didn't matter how loud I cranked my music or how much homework I had to do, I knew he was still there. And it was only a matter of time until he was yelling at Josh or complaining at Will, or knocking on my door: "Your music is too damn loud;" "your mother is cooking dinner and you need to keep the boys busy;" "I heard you told your mother you need new shoes. You know you're going to have to pay for those, right?"

So, I'd drop my stuff off, run to check with the boys, and - if they were okay - I left. At first, I stayed in the neighborhood. We didn't have cellphones back then, and I was always paranoid something would happen. I wanted to be close enough that one of the boys could find me if they needed to. But, by midwinter, I was walking for over an hour and well into the next neighborhood down along the main drag. I loved the winter sun; I loved the way I had to squint against it even as my fingers went numb in my shitty gloves and I turned frigid underneath multiple layers of clothes.

By summer, I was often gone from midday to dinner. I hated the wet, sticky heat, but my feet slamming into the pavement felt right. The sun, forcing my eyes closed, as it bounced off cars and street signs, felt both painful and good

There wasn't any sidewalk - not in the neighborhoods or along the main road - and cars flew down the narrow road. Looking back, I'd probably be terrified if you tried something similar.

But, at the time, I didn't notice the danger. Instead, I noticed how good it felt to focus - really focus - on the way I had to curve my footsteps around bramble and litter, on the sound of cars to know just how far away they were, on the trees for low hanging spider webs or bitchy blue jays. There wasn't a chance to think about how much I hated my stepdad or how scared I was that I'd somehow fail high school; I had to focus. Once, I tripped on a tree vine and tumbled into the street and was very nearly hit by a swerving soccer mom. Hilariously, it turned out to be a friend's mom and, after making sure I was okay, she yelled at me for being an idiot and drove me up to the convenience store for a snack.

The street wound past a cemetery, then some newer homes, a mega church, and some forlorn

basketball courts. After making sure I got
something to eat, she believed the lie I told her
when I said I'd use the payphone to get a ride
home, and headed off to finish her errands.
Insead, I went inside and hid in the lack of the
last aisle, soaking up the air conditioning and
steady whir from the milk case. Then, like I'd
done every day that week, I mustered up the
courage to go back.

On the hottest days, the sun could bleach my
head clean. I'd leave the store, and, by the time I
got back to my own neighborhood, all the
screaming would turn to whispers. If I was lucky,
I'd be empty by the time I got home.

***

During that first week with you, I fell back on
that old habit. Hard. Every day, I did my best to
keep us both in the safety of the sun. Your daddy
helped wrap me with the baby carrier, and I'd
tuck you deep inside. The hot June air would slap
against me, and my body, still raw at my scar and
structurally unsound, wouldn't let me get far. But,
it still felt better than inside. I'd push a few more
steps every day. Just like when I was fourteen, the
screaming in my head would settle into a dull
and ignorable rumble.

But then, a thought broke through: *god, it
would feel so good to open up these wrists and
float away.*

And I smiled.

When I got back inside, I handed you to your daddy and, with dead eyes, told him. I don't remember what he said. I only remember *failure failure failure* and waking up many hours later in our bed.

checking out

I let myself
leave. I watch
  my
     self
  drain
a
  w
ay
in the shower, and
dress the husk.
It knows how to diaper, feed,
and hold a newborn.
The baby will be fine.

A few days later, my therapist is concerned. She doesn't say as much, but I can tell from the way her skin creases around her eyes. "You've been through trauma," she tells me. "Trauma on trauma," she reminds. "Just go slow. And if something feels good and doesn't hurt anybody, you need to do it."

I nodded and whispered my horrible truth; "I don't love him. I just… don't."

"That's okay," she told me. "You don't need to. Your baby has enough love for you both right now. You will find your way."

I got off the computer to end our session and wandered slowly around the house, looking for anything that might feel... right. I noticed a pile of laundry sitting on the washer. At first, I walked by it. After all, every single book and blog I'd read was adamant that a new mom should just forget housework altogether. *Just focus on being a new mommy*, they all cooed. I wandered the two bedroom apartment only to find myself back in front of the pile.

I remembered how much Grandma had loved doing laundry.

I remembered the last time I'd spent a weekend at her apartment - long before she moved in with us. We'd gathered up the quarters and soap and bag of clothes and headed into the laundry room; it was always warm and humming in there, like a womb.

Later, when she moved in with us, I'd help her down the stairs and into the utility room. She'd sit with a cup of coffee and romance novel, switching over the loads until it was done.

The day she finally admitted she was too weak to get down the stairs was a dark one.

I refocus on the pile in front of me.

"Go ahead, sweetie." I hear her voice in my ear. "Go on then. You'll feel better when it's clean."

I shifted my weight so you were perched on my hip, then, with one hand, shoved the laundry onto the dryer and opened the washer lid. I held each piece of laundry gently: the pants I'd worn in the hospital after you were born, the shirt I'd worn on my way in, the hoodie your daddy had slept in for three days. All of it went into the cold, rushing water. Even with the lid closed, the washer's rhythmic thrumming filled the apartment. "It'll be ok ... it'll be ok ... it'll be ok."

I found a wraparound and carefully stretched it around my body. Then, I strapped you in. How could you - something so overwhelming and enormous - be so small? You nearly disappeared in the fabric folds. I took a breath and, slowly, we started cleaning the kitchen.

"Mama's little baby loves shortnin, shortnin, Mama's little baby loves shortnin bread."

I don't remember where the song came from, but it felt good on my lips. I swayed back and forth to it as I wiped the counters and started the dishes.

Over the next week, I used the housework to find some sort of rhythm. In the morning, I would put you in your bouncer and get the coffee going. Then, I'd pick up trash and clean counters and start the wash. While it whirred, we would eat. While the dryer ran, we walked. Then, you'd sleep. When it was time to put the laundry away, I put you in a bouncer in the very middle of the bed, and took my time with each article of clothes.

making friends

today, we talk politics while I
do the laundry. you sit
in your bassinet, propped up
on pillows, and babble
back as I talk Trump and Trayvon and
how violence comes in all flavors and leaves
all kinds of stains,
and why I don't talk
to my family anymore.
you squirm in the way that means
"hold me," so I do,
and we hang the last of the clothes.
I see you watching me and
for the first time,
I catch a glimpse of the familiar.

The routine settled under my skin; I was not
better, but I felt cocooned. And, I remembered,
that this is what I've always done after great
change. When all else has failed me, I always
return to routine.

***

When I first left Mom's, I found a routine
almost immediately: Dad drove me to school,
then I would survive the school day, spend the
afternoon with a friend until Dad could pick me
up, do homework, do housework, and go to bed. I
found that I could survive this way, living for an
hour at a time. Anything more than that, though,
and I stopped remembering how to breathe.

See, you aren't the first little boy I've failed, and Zero wasn't the only baby I abandoned. When I left Mom's, I still saw Josh (he was dad's kid, after all), but I wasn't allowed to see Will anymore. Or, to be more precise, I wasn't allowed to see him on my terms. Mom would dangle him on the phone; "hon, if you want to come over for a few hours, you can watch Will." Or "sweetie, we need a babysitter. Do you want to spend the night this weekend?"

Each time, I was tempted. I'd think about my surrogate baby, stuck in a house full of screaming and slammed doors. I thought about the time he ran crying to my stepdad because one of the other daycare kids had refused to share a toy and how he'd been shoved him off, and I'd helped him instead. I thought about the time Josh and I had come back after a holiday with Dad and Will had hugged me tight, crying, because "no one would play with me."

I'd plead with her to drop him off at Dad's instead, but she always refused. Angrily. I would hear her call out into her house, "Sorry, sweetie. She doesn't want to come play with you this weekend."

I'd get off the phone, shaking. "I can't go back there," I'd cry to Dad. "I'm not safe there."

But Will didn't know that. And even if he had, he wouldn't have understood.

So, I went for four months without seeing my youngest brother. When I did finally see him, at my stepdad's funeral, it was clear he no longer trusted me. I'd left him. I'd broken his heart. Repeatedly.

Your silverfish eyes reminded me of his from his own infancy, but I was determined that is all you two would ever have in common. You would never know his pain.

Promise

you, boychild, will know love.
you will know safety.
I will rip myself apart to
find it for you

There was only one problem with this promise. I had no idea how to keep it. It was all good and well to tell myself I'd do anything to give it to you, but what even was the anything I was supposed to be doing?

What the hell did I know about love?

Or safety? For goodness' sake, even after living at Dad's for a year, I was terrified that one day I'd wake up and he'd see whatever it was Mom saw and stop loving me. And I'd been right, in a way. No matter how many cups of tea I brought him, no matter how hard I tried to listen and help with his work problems, no matter how much cleaning and cooking and grocery shopping I did, I *was* unsafe, walking through a neighborhood where I did not belong. I just hadn't fully realized that truth until I was pregnant with you and it had been shoved, viciously, in my face.

Now, even after Dad had exploded at me in hatred, even after leaving for sanctuary and being covered in love by friends, even after a full year of peace and quiet in our little hobbit home, I could not shake the idea that some invisible someone was going to hurt me again. I felt as unsafe as I had ever been. A thick sense of dread covered me, smothering into my pores.

emergency session

today,
your daddy found us
on the kitchen floor.
you slept, and I shook with waves of panic.
you slept while my tears wet your skin.
you slept and I swore "I won't hurt him."
over and over
until I couldn't breathe and
the coughing woke you and
I screamed

After my panic subsided, my therapist asked me if I'd been prescribed anything new. I remembered that in the hospital, they had insisted on giving me high blood pressure medication even though we had googled - side effects may include depression and panic - and told them I was a high risk for both.

When I told my therapist, her eyes softened as she listened. "I tried to tell them my blood pressure was only so high because I hadn't slept in days and I was scared," I whispered. "I was so scared there. And then... then they said I couldn't leave because my blood pressure was too high, and then I got more scared I just... why didn't any of them listen to me?"

"You know I can't just tell you to stop taking a medication, right?" She asked, soft.

"I do," I said, "and I'll call and talk to a nurse there," I promised. "But... do you think it would be okay if I missed one dose and just tested it out?"

She confirmed I'd never had an issue before and that it was a low enough dose I could just stop. So, I did. Later that afternoon, I got the nurse's blessing, albeit begrudging, to toss the bottle.

By nightfall, the medication had worn off, and I finally settled into a neverending delicious sort of numb.

Seven

There was one silver lining to all this trauma. Unlike many new moms, saddled down with sexism and supermommy bullshit, I did not have trouble asking for help. I understood from experience: sometimes, you must resign yourself to the kindness of others. I'd been practicing that resignation for years.

When I had moved in with Dad at fifteen, I knew I wanted to keep going to my old school. There was only a year and some change left, and the idea of not seeing my friends again was unacceptable. Mom had already taken so many people from me: after the funeral, all the adults on that side of the family had gone out of their way to call and write, only to tell me what a piece of filth I was to leave my only mother while she was grieving. But my friends still loved me, and I refused to let her take them, too.

There was only one problem: I lived in a different county, over an hour away. Dad agreed to drop me off in the mornings, but I had no way to get home.

At first, I took a cab. An older gentleman with one of those tubes sticking out of his throat drove me a few times. He smelled like menthols, and he wore a faded brown wool cap. "Hiya honey." He made me uncomfortable, but it was the mostly harmless uncomfortable all young women are familiar with, and our rides were uneventful. At the end of the week, when Dad realized how much I'd spent, he told me I'd have to find another way or stop going.

"I don't understand," I said, "I mean, I told you how much it was on Monday."

"You know how tired I was," he responded. "Honestly, how did you think it would be okay to spend twenty five dollars every day getting home?" He chuckled at me. "God what did your mother even teach you about money?" He shook his head. "Get your friends to drive you and you can give them gas money. We can afford that, okay?"

So, every Sunday night, I made as many phone calls as I had to until I had a week's worth of rides. None of my closest friends had cars, so I called friends of friends, acquaintances, and people who seemed nice enough in classes.

"Hey, it's me. So I know we don't hang out much, but I got your number from Katie. I could really use a ride on Tuesday after school. What do you think? I've got gas money."

Amazingly, nobody I called ever said no. If they couldn't do a particular day, they'd take another. We never talked much on the way - I was so bogged down with depression I couldn't manage much small talk without crying - but it didn't seem to bother anyone. Some of them drove me, with the windows down and the music blasting, week after week for nearly a year.

Unfortunately, Dad kept forgetting to give me gas money. So, at first, I swore to myself I'd keep a tally and make it up to them somehow. But, after a month of rides, I realized it was never going to be possible to pay everyone back. I wasn't allowed to get a job, and I didn't have an allowance. What little money I did get for clothes or school supplies went as quick as it came. Dad was constantly complaining about child support for my brother, or the cost of raising a teenager full time, or the fact that they'd cut overtime at work. He was always scared about money. Always. The one time I did ask for gas money to help a kid who'd driven me four times in two weeks, his face went still and he asked, pointedly, if I was sure it was really worth my going to this school after all. "The whole point of this was to make things easier for you," he considered aloud, "sounds to me like this is costing you more than you originally thought it would."

So, I resigned myself to the fact that I was the poorest among my friends, and I let their parents fill their gas cards and credit cards, and I did my best not to let the shame eat me alive.

I felt that same resignation in the weeks following your birth. With every casserole, every second-hand kitchen utensil, and every gift of cash that was dropped off over the first month of your life, I was reminded of my poverty - not financial poverty (although, we were just scraping by back then), but a poverty of love. Of kindness. No one other than your daddy had bothered to take care of me since Grandma had died. It felt alien, and awful, to let myself fall into their open arms, but I had to. I had to for you. I had to let them love me so that I could spend the little energy I had trying to love you.

visitors

your grandma came today.
I watched the way she looked at you -
the way your daddy looks at you -
the way everyone
looks at you.

It's an easy expression to fake.

On the surface, I saw what they saw. You were undeniably adorable: fat cheeks and a fatter belly and a pinkness baked into your skin that reminded me of candy valentine's hearts. You were, by all accounts, delicious. But I also saw the truth of you. You weren't really mine. Or anyone's for that matter. You weren't truly here yet, still living in that space after the inhale but before the exhale.

Liminal

sometimes, right after you wake,
(and for barely a breath)
your eyes
are empty - as if

your soul forgot to drift back
from your dreams.

at night, I have to be careful not
to look directly at them.
without sunlight,
they are just
abyss.

In a way, your unnerving stare was a reminder
of my own life. Every day, I woke up in what felt
like the inbetween. My only solace was that I'd
been here once before, and, somehow, even at
fourteen, I'd found my way back to solidity. I'd
stumbled into the in-between rather on accident
back then; this was before I left Mom's, and even
before Zero. During my fourteenth summer, your
daddy broke my heart, and I needed to heal in a
way I never had before. I needed a place away
from Mom's mocking or Dad's I-told-you-so's or
so many of my friends who were your daddy's,
too. So, I went to Grandma's.

Every inch of her apartment was her own;
from the way she lined the windows with
aluminum foil for her plants, to the way she
crocheted covers for all of her second-hand
furniture. Even the floor, covered in scatter rugs,
was hers. For that reason, it was a sacred space.
Dad agreed to drop me off after she agreed to
take me in; she pulled me through the door and
into the kind of hug that nearly smothers you.

She waited all day for me to tell her what was wrong. Then, that night, as I curled into the pull out couch that smelled like old plastic and lysol, and with Murder She Wrote playing softly on her black and white television, I told her everything:

Your daddy and I had been friends for about a year by now, and over the course of that year, he became my best friend. Well, my best guy friend. We talked every day - in classes, on the phone, on the internet - and he made me feel seen in a way no one else could. I was special to him; I was the only one who could make him laugh, and I was the only one he'd loan his jacket to, and I was the only one he never tried to scam for money or food or anything else because, to most people, he was kind of an asshole. As he would tell you himself.

During our lunch hour, we would routinely break into the newspaper room and fall asleep under the tables. I was safe with him. He was safe with me.

As the school year got closer to ending, the thought of not seeing him every day cracked something open inside me. To make matters worse, I started to feel a strange sort of electricity course through me every time we touched, or bumped into one another, or happened to look into one another's eyes. Two weeks before school let out, I finally found the courage to tell your daddy how I felt about him. I cornered him in a hallway, on a Friday afternoon, just as school was ending; "Oh, by the way," I told him, mid conversation, "I really like you."

Then I ran.

Amazingly, and after the stun wore off, he called me at Dad's to tell me that the feeling was mutual. The next month was kissing and laughter and poetry and wondering if this was what it felt like to be in love. Then, it was over. He dumped me.

When she asked how he broke up with me, I told her "over email. Like an asshole. And then the next day he ran fifteen miles to make sure I was okay. That we were friends and still okay. Like an asshole."

"Sweetheart," she offered, "it sounds like he really cares for you. Try to cut him some slack. Even the best man can be a shithead sometimes."

She was right, of course. Years later, he told me he broke up with me because he knew he loved me, and he knew he wasn't ready for it, and he knew if we dated for any longer he'd break my heart so bad I'd never be able to forgive him. So, he dumped me and insisted on remaining friends. (Seriously. He was like a bad rash for weeks.)

I spent a week there, living her life instead of mine. Her apartment smelled like dollar store yarn, diabetic hard candies, and shitty instant coffee. We watched Murder She Wrote and Survivor. We ate McDonald's and sugar free ice cream. She'd nap in the afternoon, and I'd go sit in the backyard under a scraggly oak tree and watch black squirrels hop from branch to branch. I helped her do laundry and grocery shop, and she taught me to crochet and sew a button back on.

"You never know when a thing like that is useful," she'd say.

Her building was a HUD facility for retirees, and all her friends quickly became surrogate grandparents. One, Burt, was downstairs at the puzzles every day. I'd watch him and Grandma flirt back and forth and wonder: how she could be so relaxed - so at home in her skin?

I remember one evening, she turned the radio on and some old bluegrass came crackling out of the speakers. She swayed her hips while she did the dishes. "Come dance with me," she called. She extended out her soapy hands. I shook my head hard. "I don't want to drop the stitch," I told her.

The truth was, I was afraid to dance. Afraid of my body. Afraid of finding out if my hips could do what hers could. Every part of her was woman. But even with that little blip of fear, I felt safer sleeping on the floor of her one bedroom efficiency, nestled between a highway and the ghetto, than I had ever before.

My last night there, I thought about asking her to stay. But I knew there was no way. I'd been living in the space between breaths, and it had been perfect. But perfection never lasts. She hardly had enough money to feed herself, and I couldn't sleep forever on a pull out couch. Where would I do my homework? Where would I even go to school? I couldn't live her life - no matter how hard I wanted to be an eighty year old divorcee with everything figured out and a little slice of the world I could call my own. I just couldn't stay.

I still dream about it, though. Sometimes, I dream I'm back in her apartment playing double solitaire, gossiping about the building romances, and drinking crappy coffee. She's always so happy to see me, and the room smells like love.

haunted

from birth, we notice you
looking at the wall and
talking. (you are always talking and I smile at
the idea of your ideas streaming out
in words one day) but
there aren't
shadows or colors
to catch your eye, so
what is it - we ask -
or who?

It got to be a running joke by the time you were a month old. You'd look off into the dark, and we'd call out "Hi, Grandma," and I'd breathe a little easier. It was okay that I didn't love you yet because your daddy did and so did she. "You will, too," she'd tell me in my dreams. "You'll see."

witchcraft

I find myself praying over your skin

my fingers, covered in oil, trace
an invisible sigil:
you are safe
you are warm
you are loved
and everything will be ok.

A prayer for both of us, I suppose.

Eight

I pumped for two weeks. It was easy enough; for ten minutes, six or seven times a day, I did my best to imitate a dairy cow and watched, morbidly amazed at how quickly the bottles filled. It wasn't painful, like it is for so many women, nor did it lead to less milk. And unlike many infants, you seemed to prefer the bottle. Even better, you liked it straight from the fridge.

But I hated it. Sometimes, I wonder if this was my first real blush with body dysmorphophobia. At the time, I didn't know I was a nonbinary transmasculine person. I hadn't yet given myself permission to realize that I was always most comfortable wearing my brother's clothes because that's what I wanted to be - his brother. I never really wanted to be a sister at all. Even on my most feminine days, I am a tomboy looking standing next to girliness; I've always felt on the outside of their world.

But here I was: breastfeeding. I couldn't think of anything more feminine. I still can't. Even birth itself seems, somehow, more gender neutral. It was more than that, though. I hated how my breasts - once a source of such pleasure for me and any I deigned to share them with - were now for someone else's taking, and there was nothing pleasurable about it. I'd lost my bodily autonomy entirely. In this day and age, what's more feminine than that?

hostage

in the mirror, I
don't see
a woman. I only see
the violence
scraped into her skin -
every part of her
stinks
        of war

I kept asking, with increasing urgency, whether or not your daddy would be okay going to formula. From the first day we got home, he told me, "It's your body, baby. We'll get him fed however you want," but I couldn't believe him. Any minute now, he was going to realize that I wasn't fit to be a mother. Any minute now, he was going to stop lying to me that everything was going to be okay and tell me the truth: he was sick of my shit, and I needed to sack up already. After all, a good mom would sacrifice her body. A good mom would grit her teeth. A good woman would focus on the fact that I was three hundred fucking pounds and breastfeeding would help me loose the weight. But I wasn't a good woman. Or mom.

day thirteen

I take a slow walk in the sun,
but she won't hold me.
the boy sleeps between these breasts. these
bloated, bruised things tearing away from my
frame, the milk nearly ripping my skin...
I need them bloody. on the ground. caked in
dirt.
gone.
my smile is small, but dangerous.

On a lark, I reached out to your aunt, and she
confessed she hated breastfeeding and didn't do
it with any of her kids. I knew them - your
cousins. They were sweet and smart and funny
and crazy and happy. Just normal, healthy kids.
It was like the universe was screaming at me.
"Okay," I whispered. "Okay. I'll stop."
She taught me how to dry up: squeeze out just
a little bit with every pee and shower.
Immediately, I hurried to the bathroom. I
watched it go down the drain, this liquid gold,
and tried not to feel like a monster. I tried not to
think of all the other mothers out there who
were desperate that they could not make their
own.
Your daddy ran and got formula that night.
Retroactively, as I write this, I feel additional
shame knowing that many parents now are
facing a shortage. Then, though, it was easily
accessible. We read that we were supposed to try

a small amount first and see if you liked it before buying a bunch of any one brand. Like was an understatement. You wiggled in delight. You guzzled so fast and so hard that, after a few days, we had to start putting gas drops in your bottles.

I think this is what hope feels like

there's a bruise
on my left forearm. From the IV port, maybe,
but
maybe it was just another needle, or maybe
someone bumped into me or
maybe I fell and
maybe it's for the best that
I can't remember.
maybe
once it's gone
then this hole -
carved from IVs and needles and people in
masks and blue - this gaping
maw inside me ...
maybe it'll be gone too

Eventually, I worked up the nerve to tell my therapist what we'd done. I nearly cried when she told me I'd done good.

"A happy momma is a happy baby," she said, smiling.

"But I don't want to be selfish," I said. "I mean, I don't even like him. Shouldn't I at least feed him?"

"You *are* feeding him," she rebutted.

"Everyone said it would help us bond. How will we bond?" I wept openly.

She paused for a moment. At this point, we'd been working together nearly two years, and - like any good therapist - she had been careful never to share personal information. So, it caught me completely off guard when she told me, " you know. I had ppd. And I was surprised to learn breastfeeding can be a trigger. You're right; for most women, the letdown hormones make you feel all cozy. But for some? Not so much. I noticed a change once I stopped."

I nodded silently.

"You're going to bond with your baby." She raised her voice, and I felt compelled to raise my eyes and look at her. " It will happen even if you didn't want it. Stop being so damn hard on yourself already."

From down the hall, your daddy called out. "That's what I have been telling her!"

And thus The Great Dry Up began. In addition to listening to your aunt's advice, I scoured Dr. Google and found, amusingly, that cabbage leaves were supposed to help. I pulled a few refrigerated leaves out, and carefully molded them to the inside of my bra. They felt strangely wonderful, and the smell reminded me of grandma's cooking.

Throughout the day, I'd look down to see a peek of green poking out, or I'd catch a whiff of lukewarm cabbage, and giggle. It was the first thing I'd done for myself - just my fucking self - since I'd gone into the hospital.

wives tales

the sweaty green smell
of fresh cabbage
is ever present. I pack
my breasts every day, and
slowly, they deflate
from hardened fruit to gentle mounds of sand.
my nipples, exhausted
and relieved, reach
towards the floor, and I wonder
if they'll ever
be themselves again.

Spoiler alert: they never became what they were. For a good long while, they stayed hardened from their time as your food supply. When you were two, I remember getting ready for a shower and you reached up. At first, I thought it was to poke my belly button. Something that, at nearly four, you still think is hilarious. But no. "Consent is key, you cheeky monster," I sassed. But, truthfully, I hardly noticed. The mosquito bite on my shoulder hurt more. Now they are soft and tender once more, but their constant pressure on my chest is an ever present reminder of what I was: girl, woman, food. And now, when you reach up to me out of curiosity, it's repulsive in a way I can't quite articulate; I have to walk away, quickly, and remind you: "those are mine, sweetheart. No thank you."

I still haven't decided if the pleasure they can provide is worth the dysphoria they can induce. Maybe, one day, I'll know.

***

It took two full months for my milk to dry up, but I still smelled the faintest whiff of cheese waft up from my chest through to your first birthday. Now, the smell comes back a few days before each period, a harbinger of the blood about to come. It's always a reminder of what my body could do - that I could feed you - and what I was refusing to allow it to do. Some days, that feels like power. Other days, failure. Mostly, both.

empty

I push
the last few drops
of milk from my body.
they mingle with
the leftover toothpaste
in the sink. doubt collects
for a moment,

but I had to empty
these heavy breasts
to make space
in my heart
for you.

Nine

I would be the first to admit that you were mostly like every other sentient potato out there, but even at just over a month old you were unique in one particular attribute; I had never known an infant so desperate to be a part of the universe as you. You wanted to see everything, even things I knew were too far away for your young eyes to fully focus on, and you fought off sleep like a grown man might a bear. You'd thrash and scream, shaking yourself away over and over again. I found myself promising you, "nothing interesting will happen. We promise. I will be right here. Daddy will be right here." And, only after this, would you consider resting against me.

But I still couldn't call myself your mommy. More importantly, perhaps, I couldn't stand in a darkened room without slender fingers reaching from the shadows. I couldn't look at my own face in the mirror anymore, either; the eyes looking back weren't mine. I didn't worry too much about the hallucinations (they weren't trying to harm me, or you), but I knew what they meant, and I had no idea what to do about it.

Pediatrician

I can't.
I can't go...
That doctor would take one look at me
and take you.
and that would kill your daddy.

the door closes

it is so
wildly
quiet...
the dogs curl around me, licking at my hands
and tears.
their heartbeats thump out sweetly:
rest now.
rest now.

A few days after your check up, I have my own.
I was expecting my midwife from before your
birth. She was soft in a no-nonsense sort of way,
and I trusted her. But she was sick, apparently.
Instead, an incredibly slim young man with
greased back hair and a painful smile came in. He
reviewed my chart in front of me and, as he
spoke about my "routine cesarean," I tumbled
into flashbacks.
"Why are you crying?" He asked.
The absurdity of the question, asked with the
kind of docile stupidity you'd expect from a
child's toy, slapped me. I took a breath. "It was a

traumatic birth," I explained. "I still have a lot of pain."

"Oh? Hmm." Then he motioned he was going to pull my waist down far enough to see my stitching.

untitled #1

"Yes. pain is normal
but your incision is
beautiful."
he digs
his fingers in and
coos: "Such
 lovely stitching"

After he left me, still weeping, to gather myself and leave, I looked around the patient room and wondered - how many other women had been left weeping in this fucking chair? How many other mothers had a doctor respond with the same level of interest as one might a pharmaceutical commercial? I decided I'd do what I could to stop it from happening in this particular chair again. I wasn't in any shape to lead a protest or write a letter campaign, but I could make a phone call. That I could damn well do.

So, the following day, I mustered up my courage and spoke to the office manager. At first, she was polite and dismissive. I recognized her tone from when I was a customer service rep in retail. My shoulders start to tense. There was a shakiness in my ribcage that spread down through my stomach and into my pelvic floor. I hugged you tighter to me for fear of letting you fall.

"Sweetie," I offer. "I know you're doing your job. But I am high risk for ppd and postpartum psychosis. It's everywhere in my chart. I am on meds and in therapy and there is no potential harm to the baby right now. But your doctor didn't ask me a question, give me a questionnaire, or indicate - in any way - that he was actually versed in routine postpartum mental health. If I wasn't already seeing a shrink and on meds I'd be actively suicidal. You might want to get on that."

When I went back two weeks later, my regular midwife was back and deeply apologetic. She said he'd been spoken to, but who knows...

Evaluation

the midwife takes
another look
at my questionnaire: "You know,
 this isn't good,
right?"
"Yes," I nod, smiling.
"I know."

When she wheeled the medical cart over to me, my hands wrapped tightly around the sides of the bed. I did my best to breathe slowly, but each breath came out in a quick little rasp. I couldn't bring myself to lay back no matter how hard I argued with myself. Thankfully, she noticed, and she backed the cart away and out of view. We talked about nothing important while she waited for me to calm back down. Once I had, she tentatively asked if I was going to be trying for any more children anytime soon.

I laughed at her.

She suggested that I go on birth control, and we settled on an IUD. I told her that the last time one was put in, the doctor had left me alone in the surgery room for over an hour to have a panic attack by myself. "I think I might hurt myself if you all did that," I confessed. "I'm not as strong as I used to be."

She leaned over and placed a hand on my naked knee. "You seem pretty strong to me," she said. "But no. There won't be anything like that. Do you think you'd like a valium?"

My whole body smiled at the prospect.

I asked her if I'd need to take the cerivx softener again, and she assured me it wouldn't be necessary. "Women never need it after the first baby," she explained.

"I had a c-section, though," I reminded her. "Doesn't that make a difference?"

"You'll be fine," she said. "The valium will relax you."

Maybe it would have relaxed my muscles enough. But, I didn't take it. While I delighted at the idea of a pharmaceutical numb, I couldn't bring myself to fill the prescription. I was afraid of what my brain would do; would I see things during the procedure? Would I have a flashback to the c-section? I was terrified of losing control. I was terrified of them, too. Their laughter from your birthday still rang in my ears.

Besides, I reasoned, if I had taken it, then your daddy would have needed to drive me, and that seemed stupid; the place was within walking distance of our home. I didn't want him to have to schlep you and the dogs two miles back and forth just to get me.

So, I told myself I would be okay and went.

Only, it wasn't okay.

The midwife and assistant were very sweet, but my body was not interested in participating. I felt like a turkey being shoved full of stuffing. The midwife tried three different times, each one more painful than the last. After the third time, the assistant handed me a tissue and the midwife gave me a chance to stop crying before she tried again.

"I guess I should have given you the cervix softener like you suggested," she said, frustrated. "It's so unusual for women who've had babies, though. Normally it's just - pop - in you go. But you - your cervix just does not want to cooperate."

I closed my eyes and felt the shame roil up in me. I knew it. My body was wrong. I was wrong.

Dysphoria rolled over me. It was just another piece of proof to show how much I *wasn't* a mother. Not even my cervix could do it's fucking job. I was overcome with the urge to cut the whole thing out.

"Okay," she said. "We're gonna do this one more time. I'm going to tilt you back some, and you'll feel a lot of pressure."

I knew enough to know she meant pain. Pressure always means pain. I still don't understand why they always lie like that. I found a water stain on the ceiling and focused hard on it. My whole body rocked with the force of her hand. I felt something pinch inside me, then an immediate release as she removed her hand and withdrew the speculum.

"There," she said, breathless. "That wasn't so bad, was it?"

"No," I said, outside myself. I watched myself sit up on the table and take another tissue. "Not too bad at all."

To be clear, it wasn't that I wanted to lie. I didn't want to lie. Not to anyone. In fact, I was trying to be militantly honest. With everyone. I hated the idea that I knew multiple people who had been pregnant and none of them, ever, had talked about the horror show that was currently my life, and I refused to perpetuate that silence.

But I found myself in this constant push to be honest and pull not to scare anyone. I told the midwife I know I'm fucked up, but it was okay because I was in treatment. I told my shrink that I wasn't sleeping very well, but that it had been nice to have quiet time at night while you sleep. I told my friends that I was overwhelmed, but I grew up taking care of kids and I knew what to do. I told your daddy that I didn't know why I had a mental block against bathing you, but it wasn't a big deal yet. It was okay.

It's not okay

I can't bathe you.
Something (I won't say it) could happen.
and it will be An Accident. and I would be An Innocent.... but I wouldn't scream.
and your daddy
would remember all those
times I said
I'd wished we'd just gotten another dog
and leave.

Ten

When you came home, we started sleeping in shifts. I would sleep from 8pm to 1am while your daddy watched over you. Then, I'd keep you safe while your daddy slept until morning.

I'd wake up and pad quietly out to the living room; your daddy, ever the night owl, would be relaxed on the couch with you asleep in the bassinet beside him. He'd check on you one last time before I took over, and I loved the way he leaned over and stared at your sleeping face. His expression was somehow both soft and vigilant. But every time he left, no matter how quietly or carefully I curled into the sofa, you'd smell me, wake up, and demand to be fed.

It normally took an hour or so for you to fully fall back asleep, just enough to pull me completely back awake. So, while I waited, I'd sit in the dark and watch a muted television. I tried my old feel good staples, but nothing held my interest. They felt like cheap knockoffs of the original, somehow. Instead, I surprised myself by gravitating to the grittier, uglier sides of our streaming services. For once, I could watch horror unphased.

my shrink says

"It's hard to be
impressed with someone else's ghosts
when you're busy being haunted
with your own."

I think she was right, in part. But, also, I just
didn't feel much at night. All my anxieties and
insecurities were temporarily buried under a
thick blanket of gauze. Along with the rest of my
emotions. During the day, I found it
uncomfortable and fought against the numbness.
But at night?

I felt something like relief knowing the abyss
beneath my skin matched that out the night
outside. Normally, watching a child die or a
gruesome exorcism would send me sobbing and
give me nightmares for days. But now? Now, for
the first time, I found the camerawork and
wardrobe choices fascinating. I'd clock that a
character was doomed and wonder, passively,
how they were going to die. Knowing you
couldn't actually focus on the television yet, I
figured that as long as I kept the sound off, I
could keep from scaring your impressionable
brain, and I relaxed as much as I could.

I did try, from time to time, to place you in
your bassinet after you fell back asleep on me,
but my body was still too damaged. I couldn't
curve gracefully enough to set you down without
waking you back up no matter how hard I tried
or held my breath. So, I resigned myself to
curling up on the couch with you and promised

your daddy I wouldn't fall asleep. No cosleeping.
Never.

I didn't mean to

but I fell asleep with
you on my belly…
breathing
in and out
with me.
when I woke, you were
smiling, and I -
I knew
  we were safe.

For the first time, for hardly more than a
moment after waking, every cell of me knew you
were mine.

The next morning, I admitted to your daddy
what had happened. I could tell from the
darkness in his eyes that he disapproved, and I
nearly crumbled under that weight. After all,
practically the entire medical establishment is
screaming, nonstop, about the dangers of
cosleeping. But I couldn't let it go. For the first
time, I was your mother and I felt something that
I could almost call love. It was a flickering,
fleeting thing inside my chest, and I was
determined to hold on to the feeling.

But, I was crazy. Diagnosis and all. So, I didn't
exactly feel confident declaring that I knew best.
And I'd heard the horror stories. I'd read the

pamphlets and been to the webpages. Sure, families coslept in other countries all over the world, but, for whatever reason, American mothers couldn't be trusted; we'd kill our kids for sure. So, your daddy and I compromised. We would research and talk to your pediatrician and talk to my therapist. In the meantime, you slept in the bassinet, and I would keep trying to set you down without waking you up.

it's so funny I'm crying

you keep
farting yourself
awake. but it's
too damned early
for laughter.

I tried for days. Multiple times a night. Nothing worked. You woke up every time. So, we found a way for me to lay you on the couch, and I watched everything our streaming services had to offer while I sat beside you. Your daddy, a horror buff, found what I gravitated towards amusing; for the first time in our relationship, it was something we could share.

But, sometimes, I fell asleep. Just for a few minutes each time. Every time, though, it was as if my body trusted it more, and it got harder and harder to stay awake. Harder and harder to sleep away from you.

A few nights in a row, your daddy waited until after your last feed and got you settled down again for me. I'd lay down on the couch and drape my hand into your cot. I could hear you breath in and out, in and out, and I should have been able to fall asleep beside you. But I could hardly bear to close my eyes.

what if

"if" you wake up. not when.
I stand over the bassinet and
what if ...
what if the universe hears me? heard me
whisper to his father in the dark? :
            "We shouldn't have done this.
            I miss everything about me that's
gone."
I gather you up and nest your
weight into the soft of me.
please (i beg)
I only sort of meant it.

I had to be holding you. I had to feel you breathe. That's now I knew you were safe. Then, I could sleep.

***

A full eighteen months later, even as you turned two years old, I struggled to sleep if I couldn't feel your stomach rise and fall. I worried something would happen. But, instead of suffocating, I worried you would have a nightmare and wake up terrified and alone. I worried that in the sixty seconds it would take me to hear you and come running, you will feel unloved. And that is sixty seconds was sixty seconds too many.

Still - I promised your daddy.

During a telephone consult, the pediatrician was indifferent. I didn't drink or take sleeping pills, so she didn't care. But my therapist thought it was a brilliant idea. Since you didn't seem to trigger me as much at night anyway, she thought it was a low risk way to bond. We discussed the safety measures, we talked about the risks, and I told your daddy everything. He asked for a compromise; try to get you to nap on your own during the day, try to start you in the bassinet at night. But, if you woke up, we'd cosleep. I happily agreed.

I dutifully put you down for every nap, and I even managed to keep you sleeping once. But only once. I set you down so carefully, curtains drawn and white noise blaring, and went to do something I had not done in nearly a month: pee by myself. It was strangely luxurious. I remember feeling so proud of myself, and thinking that your daddy would be proud. I was finally learning how to handle this all.

But when I came back to check on you, there was spitup pouring from your nose and mouth. Your little lips, stretched wide in a silent scream, were turning blue. I snatched you up, faced you to the floor, and watched as your vomit splattered onto the floor. The wet thud was immediately replaced by your screams.

I have never been more thankful for that sound.

While I used my shirt to clean your mouth and nose, I apologized over and over. "Never again," I promised. "You'll never sleep alone again."

Your daddy, who'd been out at a meeting, came home to find us on the couch. I think I was in the same stained shirt. You were asleep in my arms. When I told him what happened, he googled and told me it isn't possible for babies to choke on their own spit up unless there's medication involved, and you were on none.

"I know what I saw," I told him. My whole posture dared him to argue.

He nodded silently.

***

By the time you turned three, I had mostly learned to trust the universe. On the rare days that you napped, you did so all by yourself in your bed. Some nights, you'd fall asleep on your own, too, and I would sneak in after a blessed hour of trash television and chamomile tea. After all, you were 35 lbs and over three feet tall. The bed felt ever smaller, and, truthfully, I missed the solitude of falling asleep alone. Even if 'alone' was beside you on the floor.

Now, you are nearly four, and I fully believe that, should you need me, your lungs would wake me from three blocks over. More importantly, I believe that you know that even if it takes sixty seconds for me to force myself awake and rush to you, you know I will come. I will be there. Always.

I'll confess, though; sometimes, I miss curling my body around yours on our little mattress on the floor. Waking up with the sun, cuddling and cooing as we listened to music and birdsong, was sometimes the only bright spot in those early days. Currently, you're going through a bit of a rough patch, waking up at night with gas or nightmares, so my body is getting accustomed to sleeping on the floor once again. I miss sleep, and I miss my bed, but I know that in the next few years, you will long for privacy: there will come a time when it is the last time I sleep on your floor. Now that I love you, I am achingly aware.

So, I do my best to savor it and prepare myself to hear you when you're ready.

three a.m.

we are squirrels, curled into our nest.
you settle against me and
we sink
into a careful Haven
of soft and
down.
the world is quiet... dark... a   sleep.

Eleven

Looking back, it's strange. Once you were born and out in the world, it took so long to recognize you. But, the moment I knew you were inside me, I loved you. And I knew almost immediately. Three weeks into your existence, I fell off a rock climbing wall and dislocated my elbow. Sitting in a cheap metal chair in the middle of a crowded indoor climbing center, in an almost hilarious amount of pain, I remember thinking, "I'm fucking pregnant. Shit," just as your daddy popped my bone back in the socket. I can't tell you how I knew. I just did. I didn't tell anyone, though. Not even your daddy. For a few precious days, I had you all to myself.

Eventually, I got to the grocery store and purchased a test. After it confirmed what I already knew, I called out to your daddy from the toilet. "Babe, I've got something to show you."

"In the bathroom?" I could hear his squeamishness from across the basement.

"Yes."

He peeked his head into the little purple room, and I offered up the test to him. Then, I watched his eyes go wide and his mouth lift up into a smile as he realized that I was showing him two little blue lines: the start of our family.

After I told him, I made your daddy promise that we would wait to tell anyone else. But I

couldn't wait for more than another day to tell
Dad. There were many reasons for that, but as a
matter of practicality, he was bound to notice
during those first three months while we waited
to tell everyone else. So, later that day, after a
celebratory decaf latte, your daddy and I went
into his room, hands held tightly, to offer up the
wonderful news. It came out in a rush, "you're
going to be a grandpa! Isn't that wonderful?"

foreshadow

when you were in my belly,
my father asked us:
what did we want
for you?
   You taught me to survive (I said),
   but I want more -
   I want him to thrive.
he jeered our ambition with the smile
he saves for solicitors and complained
over my ungrateful tone.

I guess I thought I had a good relationship
with my dad because, unlike most of the other
dads that I knew who were always at work or
irritated at their daughters, *my* dad always made
me feel special. Important. In my first memory of
him, I am hardly five and my parents could not
have been divorced more than a year, but they

were divorced - not separated - and he was dropping my brother and I back off at Mom's.

In my memory, he is kneeling on the white tile of the entryway. I go to take my hand away from his, and he starts sobbing. Immediately, I turn back to him and curl my little arms as tight around his neck as they will go. "It's ok, Daddy. It's ok."

As I got into elementary school, we got into the habit of talking on the phone every night. I'd tell him about what I was learning, who I sat with at lunch, how dinner went. And, to his credit, he treated each piece of information as valuable as gold. I'd hear my stepdad on the other side of the door, barking orders at one of the boys, and close my eyes to pretend I wasn't just on the phone with Dad, but I was there in his quiet little apartment. I'd pretend I was curled up on our beat up oversized couch that smelled like incense and tiger balm, with the television on low in the background, and our jungle of weeds poking out from the balcony's open sliding door.

By the time I was in middle school, he was telling me about his day, too. Often, we'd spend more time talking about his day than mine. I knew the names of all his coworkers, and I felt so proud - so puffed up - when he asked for my advice. My dad managed a dozen people and needed *my* help. None of my friends even knew what their dads did let alone *helped* them. I'd roleplay asking for a coworker's assistance, or help sift through options for dealing with his dick of a boss. I wasn't just some eleven year old. I was a confidante. He even started letting me proofread his technical papers; "you're such a good writer," he'd tell me, "and smarter than half the guys on my team."

Sometimes, Mom would ask what we talked about for so long, and I relished the look of jealousy in her eyes when I'd say "nothing."

Unlike her, he always wanted to spend time with me. He did Josh, too, but it never seemed to matter as much to Josh as it did to me. My best friend's dad had to be dragged to any extracurriculars, but mine? He came to every softball game and practice, driving an hour both ways. Afterwards, we'd go for McDonald's ice cream or just hang out in the car for a few minutes. I played for years - all through middle school - and he never missed a game.

Towards the end, I injured myself pretty good. I was at bat and swung when I shouldn't have; the ball grazed across my hand and pulled my thumbnail clean off. No one saw the injury, just that the ball caught me. I walked to first and made it, over the course of the next few players, all the way home. When I got back to the dugout, my hand was covered in blood. I still remember how proud Dad was when I told him I wanted to keep playing. "That's my kid," he beamed to the other parents. He was just as proud when I told him about kicking the crap out of the boy down the street.

When I was older - high school and beyond - we'd go on lunch dates. The waitresses would giggle at how cute we were. Or, occasionally, they'd glare at us, thinking Dad was my husband and I his little trophy wife. It always felt good to hear that. Now, of course, it's a bit nauseating that I liked to hear it so much, but I think I understand why: Dad had always made a show of never dating, never even thinking about dating because, he'd say, he didn't want any other person getting in between him and his kids. He wasn't going to do to me what Mom had done; he wasn't going to force some asshole into my life just because he couldn't stomach being alone. He was choosing his kids. He was choosing me. I was the closest to a wife he would ever allow himself.

Writing it now, the dysfunction of it all feels so shameful. It's also a bunch of bullshit. Dad wasn't choosing to stay single; he'd been married twice before my own mother and had a self-reported shitty history of relationships. He'd been a terrible boyfriend, lover, husband, and everything in between. Of course, I didn't know that then, though. I only knew that he made me feel seen and understood and special in a way that Mom had never even bothered to try.

Once, when I was still in elementary school, he went with my class on a field trip to the aquarium. All the other moms were eager to point out how "amazing" and "wonderful" it was that my Dad, not my Mom, was there. I remember that one kid, Chris, forgot to bring money for the gift shop. Without embarrassing him, Dad offered him ten dollars - just enough for a key chain.

No one else would have thought it was a big deal, but I knew better. I knew how much Dad paid for child support, and how hard he worked to make sure we had our own set of everything at his house. He told us every time we went clothes shopping, or shoe shopping, or for school supplies. "No kid of mine is going to drag clothes back and forth in a duffle bag," he'd say. "I don't care if I have to put it all on credit cards."

Ten dollars was a lot of money, and he spent it on one of my friends for me. Mom would have never.

He always bought the best gifts, too. After I left Mom's, she stopped with the gifts entirely, and Dad seemed to take the responsibility of making up for that seriously. He rarely got what I asked for. Instead, he'd offer a gorgeous birthstone ring, or a beautiful leather bag, or an expensive set of art supplies I'd always thought about but been afraid to ask for. Somehow, it was always exactly what I wanted.

Even during the lean years, when I was first living with him and paying for gas with change, he made sure I felt special - and seen - on birthdays and Christmases. And he would help Josh, too, pick out something that was just... perfect.

When I was in my twenties, he started missing the mark: a sweater that wasn't my style, or a bracelet that was cheap and poorly made. Then, the last two years before we left, he didn't buy me anything at all. Towards the end, I bought myself a pretty pair of earrings and had your daddy give them to him to give to me. I told myself he was just too weak and forgetful from illness, and this would help him save face. I couldn't bear the truth; he was buying all sorts of things online and he remembered dates just fine. He bought things for Josh, and even for your daddy's birthday without any prompting. For whatever reason, when it came to me, he just didn't care.

Sometimes, I search through my memories looking for the exact moment when he decided it was too much trouble to love me. I mean, it's not like he stopped the awful stuff. I might feel differently if he went from sometimes loving me and sometimes hating me to a sort of overall tepid indifference. Like, if the price of no longer getting told I was an incompetent nitwit was that I stopped getting shiny gifts or taken out for dinner on my birthday, I probably would have accepted that arrangement. But that's not what happened. He didn't stop screaming at the dogs or punching walls or telling me I'd never make it as a writer. Only the good times stopped. The sparkly bits of our relationship, one by one, just faded away.

My therapist would ask me to consider just how sparkly those bits really were. She'd remind me that the "out of the blue" flowers he brought home almost always came on the heels of ugliness. She'd ask me to refocus; instead of fixating on how often he attended my games, I might consider all the times I only attended them in the first place because he forced me to. She'd remind me that the first panic attack I can recall was while begging him to stay home from a basketball game, and how I routinely worked myself up to near vomiting before big softball games.

But even after all this time, and with everything I know about narcissism and love bombing, those memories still feel... hallowed. Sacred. And I am still, after years of no contact and healing, heartbroken he will never make me feel that way again.

sweet boy

my eldest dog
rushes
to lick the tears
from my face before
they can fall.
with a paw on either shoulder,
he hugs me every time
I cry.

(considering how often I catch him eating shit,
my feelings on this are mixed.)

Twelve

day 47

we're walking every day now,
and you thrash
in delight
at the sounds of traffic
and wind.
my body
nearly envelopes you,
and it's the first time it makes sense:
I am your mountain. thunderous with
every step. flesh enough
to protect you.

I decided to stop trying to convince myself
that I was your mother. I was sick of crying over
something I could not. I focused, instead, on your
safety and comfort. I could do that; I could keep
you safe, keep you fed, keep you rested. I could
even keep you happy for the most part. It was
exhausting and repetitive and often incredibly
uninteresting, but I could do it. I couldn't be your
mother, but I could be a damn good caregiver. I
would do my job, and I would do it well.

But throughout the day, every day, there
would come a moment - a lull - and the weight of
my missing motherhood made the nerve endings

around my c-section scar scream and carved a
bloody mess in my chest, and I would double
over with a sob so fierce I had to clamp my hands
over my mouth to keep from scaring you. It hurt
too much. It hurt every time I picked you up and
felt... nothing.

internet forums

well meaning women -
"one day,"
they tell me I won't remember.
It "will fade,"
they tell me. "like a dream."
I want to wake up.

I kept asking my shrink: How can it hurt to be
numb? What is the point of not feeling anything
more than skin deep if this empty maw of ache
and need is somehow still breaking through?
What the fuck is the point?

After a few days, I started to feel guilty. I
hadn't told your daddy about my giving up. I
hadn't told him I was pretty sure I was never
going to really be your mommy, that I was
resigned to simply making sure you never knew
my horrible truth, and that I'd have to rely on
him to fully love you. The idea of telling him sent
me dry heaving, but keeping it from him felt like
the worst sort of lie. When I finally found the

courage to tell him, I did so while rocking back and forth in a corner of the linoleum kitchen floor.

I was so sure he'd leave me.

I would have left me. A thousand times, I would have. Anything to make sure you always felt loved.

confession

He's not mine. He's cute and sweet and I think it's funny that he sort of laughs when he farts and I like hanging out with him
    but
    he's just... not
"yet," you say. "He and I will
    wait right here."

He held me on that floor until you screamed for attention, then picked you up and brought you over with him. He nestled you into his lap, then reached back over to hold me close. I remember you reached up to play with the ties on my sweatshirt as my tears fell over your hair, and I watched your fingers dance in the air until the panic and pain settled back into a quiet numb. All the while, your daddy held us both and waited.

And then, very shortly thereafter, a funny thing happened.

I felt something.

I want to burn it down

we're watching
The Handmaiden's Tale.
(maybe not the best for a baby but
whatever because I cannot stop it now.)

I am delighted and terrified by
my rage.

I was angry. I was filled with it, and it felt so
amazing to be filled with something - anything
other than the hollow howling wind and vast
cold water that had been living in my chest for
weeks now. I was warm again. Alive. On fire in
the most perfect sort of way. I was suddenly
angry at damn near everyone - my mother, my
father, my brothers, the doctors and midwives
and nurses, society for it's fucked up notions of
motherhood and maternity leave and for not
requiring some sort of competency test for
people to have children - I shook with it. Fueled
with it, I turned the television off and cleaned the
entire apartment, then I baked cookies, and went
walking farther with you than I ever had. It was
the most powerful I'd felt in months.
　　During the night, my dreams took that rage
and broke it down, exposing what I'd been too
afraid to feel all this time - the grief that I'd tried
to drown under all my numbing. I woke up with

tears dried on my face and a fullness in my chest.
Grief had bobbed up to the surface and settled
into me like a bag of wet sand, dripping cold and
heavy on my bones.

my hips

are still birthing
wide. I imagine
they are two
outstretched hands, searching. aching (in
every step). waiting
for you
to arrive.
(i guess) because it's so
hard to fathom
you are mine.
you are mine.

(you are,
aren't you?)

    I'm not sure a person can ever really be
ready for grief, but I expected, as I felt it settling
into my chest, that my body was finally ready to
grieve the loss of my father. I figured maybe I
might have to contend a bit with losing Grandma,
too, as she only died a couple years before, and I
was even ready to grieve your birth and how it
had been nothing like I'd hoped, or been
promised. But none of those sorrows were the

first to ooze out of this bag of wet sand now situated securely between my breasts. They would all come later. Even though I hadn't had a meaningful relationship with her in decades, I was completely overcome by a deep grief for Mom.

When I was young, I adored her the way most little girls do their mothers. I even tried to name my guinea pig after her in a show of devotion. After all, she was everything I wasn't: tiny-waisted, fearless, funny, and crass in an unapologetically charming sort of way. Whenever we went anywhere, she'd run into someone she knew. And she was a master code switcher. Everyone felt comfortable around her.

Everyone but me.

I didn't realize until I was much older that she actually wasn't fearless at all. It's true that she gave very few fucks about what people, on average, thought of her. At the same time, though, she was plagued by a darker version of the anxiety I now carry. After all, her mother was actively monstrous. Mine was just ... uninterested. Absent. I spent my life feeling unloved. She spent hers feeling hated.

I tried at least a half dozen times over the last twenty years to find a way back to her, but it never stuck. Each time I tried, she was smaller somehow. Frail. Afraid. The last time I saw her, nearly a decade ago, her eyes clocked me as if I was a wildfire coming to devour her whole.

In my head, I'd try to approach her the way one would a wounded animal, doing everything I could think of to show her I meant no new harm. But I could never seem to apologize enough, or correctly, for leaving all those years ago.

No matter how much I tried, or how small I worked to make myself, conversations would inevitably drag back to how I left her alone when she needed me most; my stepdad had been diagnosed with stage four brain cancer shortly after I'd left, and I had refused to come home to be nursemaid to a man who had spent my entire life making his contempt for me clear. My grandparents and aunt and great-aunts had all rallied around her, sending me emails and phonecalls to let me know that I was an "ungrateful child," "heartless," and "a useless cunt," for leaving her to take care of her dying husband all on her own. Yet they, for some reason, owed no apology to me.

Once, after one of my later attempts - she'd reached out shortly after my marriage and we had managed an awkward lunch - she sent me a birthday card from the Holocaust museum. "I wish you well," it said, "but all you do is hurt me. I don't want to know you anymore." I remember that I had to sit down from laughter as I stared at this depressing ass ballerina that some encampment survivor had drawn. "Who sends a birthday card from the Holocaust museum? Why the fuck do they even sell cards?"

The last time I'd had any contact with her was at my brother's wedding. We'd been in the same room together for the bridal shower, and it had been cordial, so I figured the day itself would be fine. But, of course, I was wrong. She nearly made me miss the photos, she tried to steal my corsage, and she actively rushed away whenever I was more than five feet near her. I found out later she told his fiance's family that she had no idea who I was or why I was there and that the bride had needed to fill them in.

Now, it was more than five years after that day, and I could not stop missing her, or wishing for her voice. I ached in a way I hadn't since I was a child. I started to wonder: should I reach out? Maybe the reason she'd been so cruel to me when I left was because she couldn't stomach that I'd left her home for *his*.

After all, I knew their marriage had been dysfunctional. But, somehow, that it was abusive had never clicked until after I had left him myself. This was in part, probably, because Mom didn't talk about their marriage very often. She actually did a pretty good job of staying neutral about Dad in front of us kids. But after a particularly joyful Thanksgiving, drunk on boxed wine, she giggled about how, "He kept punching holes in walls. And I was sick of it. So, I started making it expensive for him. For every hole he punched, I broke a few plates." At the time, I didn't understand why she only talked about things like that when she was drunk, and I certainly didn't understand the uneasy looks on the other adult faces in the room. But now - now I understood. He'd punched walls around me, too.

I thought about you. If you suddenly told me you were going to live with my father, would I be clear headed enough to tell you why it was a terrible idea? Or would I just shut down... raging and heartbroken that you'd choose someone like that over me?

Is that what she had done?

I had so many questions. Not just about her past, or ours, but about everything. About you. Every day you grew bigger, a reminder that while she was there for Will's child, and while she knew everything about Josh's stepkid, she wouldn't be there with me. And she wouldn't know you.

It was grief on grief on grief.

mom

I catch her in my arm -
the way it curls, cradles
the boy.
     and I hear her
all the time in
his lullaby:
       abi yoyo, abi yoyo,
       abi yoyo bi yoyo bi yoyo...
and I wonder
if she felt so lost when she
had me.

There was something comforting about the grief, though. Even now, after years of therapy, I still don't fully understand how feeling so much loss could keep propelling me forward. I don't understand how the swell of sadness that would rise up in my stomach a few times a day could jar me out of my numbness just enough to focus me on the moment at hand. But somehow, miraculously, it did. Then, the sorrow would step aside for a few seconds, and, for just a few seconds more, I would see you.

almost familiar

I watch your soul
settle - a little more
solidly every day.
it stares out into this
strange, exasperating world with
calm, discerning eyes that, for a moment, remind me
of grandma. But
you're not her,
and
I find myself
unsettled... reminded
you
are a Stranger.

Thirteen

I have always thought it was darkly funny that you decided to be a summer baby.

Sure, technically you were born in the spring, but by the time the bruises from birth had disappeared from your skin, it was summer, and I have always hated the summer. I can remember complaining about it even as a kid, and I maintain it is a miserable season (the house is impossible to clean, everything is always damp, you need a change of clothes after the mailbox, and the holidays are garbage. Come at me).

So, I think it's kind of hilarious that the universe was all *'oh, you're really uncomfortable in eighty degrees? Here. have a baby. That'll fix it.'*

Amusingly, you are no fan of the heat either. Your daddy, on the other hand, loves summer, so this is the first thing you and I share, and I relished the bond. I started having to wear long sleeved tee shirts because you hated how your cheek would get all sticky against my skin. If your bottle wasn't ice cold, you screamed. Still, I had to get outside. I had to walk. So, in order to get up and out before the swelter of midday, I carved us a new routine.

small mornings

we wake
when your daddy
brushes his teeth. we turn
the kettle on, then
I set you in your rocker. You
bounce while I sing.
    "Mama's little baby loves
       shortening, shortening,
      Mama's little baby loves
       shortening bread..."
I warm your bottle,
prep the French press,
and feed the dogs.
It's the same every morning:
a routine
small enough to
wrap my hands around
but big enough
         to breathe.

For the most part, your daddy was still
working at home. He was only on paternity leave
for two weeks, but his boss agreed to remote
work when he realized I was unwell. In this, we
were enormously privileged.

    But starting in August, twice a week or so, he
had to go in.

change is coming

"Tomorrow," I tell you,
"It'll just be us.
But we'll be okay. Right?"
you look up at me
from your playmat
with those silvery eyes,
and we stare into each other until
you burp.

I spent the week before your daddy headed
into work frenzying myself into a bigger and
bigger panic. But, as usually happens, when the
day came around, I was calm. I crushed the panic
into a tiny diamond and set it away on a shelf
somewhere, as I'd been taught by both parents to
do. Besides, it was exciting, in a way. After years
of caregiving, first for my grandma and then Dad,
I had not been alone in an incredibly long time. I
think, maybe, it could have been an
overwhelming kind of quiet, but between you
and the dogs, there was just enough noise.

together on the couch

I can't feel my arm and I've had to pee for ten
minutes, but yeah.
    I think
    I might
    be
    sort of
    glad

you exist.

Without your daddy home, I found myself
unexpectedly braver. I realized that if I
positioned your bouncer on the table just so, you
could sit upright and watch me make coffee. You
were thrilled with the new vantage point, and I
could get away without holding you for long
enough to drink half of it. If I coiled my
pregnancy pillow inside your bassinet, you could
sit up and watch me fold laundry, and that would
entertain you long enough for me to finish.
Every day your daddy left, I would dare myself
to try something new. I wasn't ready to walk the
dogs while wearing you, but I would pack you in
your stroller and roll it out the back door, where
you'd watch the dogs dig and play. Holding their
leashes loosely, I'd get them to run and leap in
circles like a ringmaster in the world's cheapest
circus. There was just enough shade back there
that we could while away most afternoons with
the sounds of sirens and traffic in the
background.

grounding

I want to
lay your body
down on this dirt, so
you know
from where you come.

but this grass is more glass than green.

I pick a few blades, help
you hold them,
and marvel at how delicate
your fingernails are.

Towards the end of the month, I got your
daddy's permission to try to walk you and the
dogs together. Normally, I wouldn't bother to ask,
but I felt I needed his okay in case I tripped and
killed us all or something. (Considering that I
have an established history of falling and/or
hurting myself in truly stupid accidents, it was a
valid concern.) So, first, I tried while he was
home. It was just a few minutes out and back, but
between the leashes, poop bags, treats and you in
the carrier, I felt like I was prepping for Everest.
It took longer to get out the door than it did to
actually walk. After a few tries, though, I
streamlined things, and it wasn't long at all
before we were walking nearly half a mile all by
ourselves.

baby's first bath

your pink cheeks,
slick with sweat and screaming,
shame.
    how dare I
drag you out under the sun

just because I need to see the sky.

I soak a towel in lukewarm water,
and kiss it gingerly along
your thighs,
your hands,
your face.
"please. forgive me."

And then, just like that, it was September. You
were three months old. It was unbelievable. We
had survived the fourth trimester. We were
surviving.

we're drenched

in daylight and sweat.
A car speeds by, and the breeze
sends you kicking with laughter.
"Car," I whisper,
"vroom."

Fourteen

friends stop by

they hold you, dance you, bounce you, and I'm relieved to have
my body be
mine again.

before they leave, though, my arms ache for holding
your small body against my stomach. your
breath on my skin, your hand on my chest, is exactly
what I need to feel.

Most kids hate trading in the sunburned idleness of summer for homework and early wakeups, but there is something about September that has always soothed me. I loved all the back to school rituals. I still do. I haven't been a student, or teacher, for nearly a decade now, but just last week I found myself in an office supply store, wandering down the aisles with reverence. I am always the most myself when there is a chill in the air.

As proof, all the big events of my life have happened in the fall; I fell in love with your daddy, I left Mom's, and I learned about you. And while I did not leave my father's until early spring, the seed of knowing I would have to sprouted that November.

By then, Dad had been sick for years. It had started legitimately enough, with a severe case of something like food poisoning and a persistent chest pain nobody could diagnose. Over the course of that first year, I dragged him to every type of specialist we could get an appointment to. Sometimes, they'd notice something specific enough to treat. Other times, not. Most often, they would ask lifestyle questions and he would lie.

At first, even though he lied about what kind of food he ate or how much he exercised, he seemed willing to listen to their advice. If it had been food poisoning, they said, he'd best be served by trying an elimination diet and reintroducing foods slowly.

Since both the gastroenterologist and the cardiologist said it seemed his chest pain was a severe kind of heartburn and GERD, they were adamant that he should act judiciously as if that was the case. If after a month of carefully following the lifestyle protocols and taking the medications, he was still in distress, they would consider more invasive testing. I watched him nod politely and, at first, thought he meant it.

After each appointment, we would come home, he'd nap, and then we would go over my notes together. And, like he had in the office, he agreed to change his diet for the sake of scientific discovery.

He seemed to understand that they couldn't do anything else until they ruled this out, and the only way to rule this out was to be a good patient and do as the doctors said. So, I threw out all the junk, bought everything we needed for a GERD diet, and cooked everything from scratch for the next few days. But after those few days and with only mild improvement, he refused to fight his food cravings anymore.

"It's not worth living this way," he lamented. "Fuck the doctors. I'm not letting them take the one good thing left in this shitty life."

So, I threw out all my cooking and ordered him fast food.

Even now, writing this, I have an incredible amount of compassion for him during all of this. I've struggled with emotional eating on my own, and I know how difficult it can be to unlearn. I'm still unlearning it. I have dealt with chronic physical and emotional pain, and I know how bleak they can make the world seem.

I understand why he would be compelled to make the choice for short term joy and eat the hamburger or drink the milkshake as opposed to the long term joy of physical health. I understand now, and I understood then. But that didn't make the hurt any less; it was still a special kind of killing to know that my father took more happiness from a fast food milkshake than he ever did me.

For months, I watched him cycle; go to a doctor, eat better for a few days, binge, and be terribly ill, swear he was done eating like shit and ask to go to the doctor again. It was as if I was stuck in an eating disorder version of "Groundhog's Day," and I could not figure out how to get out. I did, once, get him to admit he was going to kill himself with how he ate. He'd been suffering with heartburn and GERD for the better half of a day, unable to keep anything down except a few bites of bread. It was the lowest I had ever seen him. "Okay," he said, near tears. "You win. Sign me up for therapy, hypnosis, a life coach, whatever you want. I don't want to feel this way anymore."

I went downstairs and made a flurry of appointments, so proud of him - he'd finally hit rock bottom and was ready - and excited he was going to be able to finally find a path back to better. But the following morning he demanded I cancel them all. So, I did. And at follow up appointments with the rest of the doctors, I watched them clock his lies and do what I could not: offer medication and wash their hands of him.

Unlike lifestyle changes, he did agree to medication. He was reticent at first, concerned he'd be a zombie, but by the end of the year, he was on benzos, opioids, and using marijuana. It did not turn him into a zombie, nor did it diminish his mental capacity. Frankly, it did something worse. Whatever mechanism he had held on to that reminded him to mask - to at least act like a decent person to me from time to time - disappeared. It felt like, overnight, he just forgot how not to be cruel.

It started with the marijuana.

Even though it wasn't yet legal in our state, my brothers used and grew it, so access wasn't a problem. Nor was money. The problem was that it was illegal; your daddy was a government contractor, and if he knew there was an illegal substance in his home, and someone found out that he knew, he could lose his job. It was the first time I was forced between the two of them in a consequential way.

Dad feigned understanding whenever your daddy was in the room, but the minute he left, his tone would change. "I can't believe you are really talking about my not taking something that's completely safe and might actually help me feel better," he'd bellow at me. "Are you really going to be that selfish?"

When I explained my concerns again, he offered, flippantly, "just lie to him."

So, I did.

And I hated myself for it.

I didn't just hate myself for lying. I hated myself for compromising my marriage when it didn't even work. It would have been one thing if Dad had agreed to my requests to only use upstairs, to only use with the windows open, and to only use when your daddy was out of the house. But he respected exactly none of those rules, and I was constantly spraying air freshener, reopening windows, and putting his supplies out of sight.

On top of that, he was constantly trying to get me to join him. Every time I reminded him to open the window wider while I was in the room, or tell him I was too busy to sit with him any longer, he'd tell me I just needed to relax and blow a big puff of smoke in my direction. When I did have time to sit upstairs with him, he thought it was hilarious to covertly close the window and hotbox me against my wishes. This happened multiple times.

Each time, I would find myself incapacitated for the rest of the day because marijuana completely ruins my vision and I lose all sense of depth perception. Then, at the end of the day, Dad would chastise me for failing to get done whatever errands needed doing.

After a few times of me complaining to my brother, he decided he'd advocate on my behalf for Dad to try edibles instead. He had a friend who had an out-of-state hookup, and I knew Dad had the money for it. On top of that, edibles would be a hell of a lot easier to hide from your daddy than smoke, so I encouraged Josh to reach out. He came over one afternoon and mentioned that Dad could get a more effective high from edibles.

"Oh, that would be great," Dad agreed. Then, he turned to me, "and you are such a great cook. I bet you could figure out how to make butter."

I turned to Josh for help. "But, I thought you had a guy. I mean, I've never done anything like that before. It's gotta be tricky, right? I don't want to waste product."

Before Josh could respond, Dad jutted in, angry. "Don't be ridiculous. I'm not shipping something across state lines. You know, for someone who always says they're worried about their husband's job... Besides," his tone turned light again, "you love all that kitchen shit. You can make cookies and brownies. It'll be fun."

"It's really not that hard," Josh offered. "And Taylor already said he'd do half price on the first batch so you can play around."

So, I agreed.

It was simple enough to cook during the day when your daddy was at work, and after an ill-fated attempt where I breathed in too many fumes and was rendered useless for an afternoon, I figured out how to coordinate the windows and the exhaust fan. But Dad seemed determined to rub your daddy's nose in it; he left cookbooks out on the main floor, he "forgot" a half-empty container of cookies on the kitchen counter instead of taking them upstairs, or, when we were all watching television together upstairs, he'd pull out a piece of cookie and tease your daddy about how he shouldn't ask for one.

I think I might have felt less awful about the position we were putting your daddy in if it had resulted in any kind of warmth or appreciation from Dad. But, the cookies were always too crunchy or too soft. They were never potent enough; didn't I know he was in pain? Why was I "pussyfooting around?" They tasted too gingery, or he'd want a different kind than I had made. Or he'd get frustrated at getting cookies all the time and wonder when I was going to figure out brownies. It was always something.

One time, at his insistence, I rushed the process. Instead of making the butter and letting it sit for a few days, I made the butter in the morning and the cookies in the afternoon. I spent all day in the kitchen. My fingers stank. My hair stank. I was famished because I'd been scared to eat anything accidentally cross-contaminated while I was actively cooking, and I was freezing from cooking with all the windows open on a forty-degree day.

At first, he offered a wide smile as I handed him a still warm chocolate chip cookie. He took a bite, wrinkled his nose, and glared at me. "What did you do to these," he asked.

"You said yesterday that you wanted to cut out dairy," I said, timid. "You thought it was making you worse."

"Jesus. I didn't mean out of the cookies," he groaned. "And did you even put in the pot? I keep telling you to make them stronger." He took another bite and sighed. "I guess they'll have to do."

As he continued to eat one and started on another, I watched his body relax and his eyes haze over. Obviously, they were strong enough. "God," he said, looking up at me. "You look like hell. I keep telling you not to work so hard, but you never listen, do you sweetie?"

"I guess not," I said. I remember my body relaxing as I realized he was starting to relax enough to sleep.

"Yup. I know. No one knows you like I do. Did I tell you today that I love you?"

"No," I said, forcing a smile at the familiar refrain, "I don't think you did."

***

I did not understand it at the time, but my father is a clinical narcissist. That term gets thrown around a lot these days, but he wasn't a person with narcissistic tendencies. He was, and still is, a true narcissist. Narcissists learn, very early on, to wear masks. It's the same mechanism that makes us think serial killers are just the men next door. As I've said before, my father's illness, and his steady stream of medication, ripped away his mask. For me, there was no hiding from what was underneath: an empty, angry, self-important, never-satisfied need.

When I was not quite three months pregnant with you, on a damp November night, I sat on the floor and rocked silently as your daddy and mine screamed. Dad had been discharged from the hospital for a near heart attack and when we had gotten home, Dad was in an unusually pleasant mood from all the not dying. The two of them had been teasing one another and then I had joined in. I had made a joke. Something about soda.

Shortly thereafter, we had gotten him settled upstairs and your daddy and I went out for food. When we came home, I was summoned. "I need to talk to you," he texted. I thought maybe he was feeling ill, or something was wrong with his meds. But no. How dare I, he seethed, make that sort of joke. "Who the fuck do you think you are?"

He must have been berating for longer than usual because your daddy came up to find me sitting down across the room from my father, as far as I could get, trying to make myself as small as possible.

We were up there, in that fetid room, for hours. I don't remember much of it, but at some point I choked out, " I've always known what you are. I know the stories. But... you used to at least try to be sweet to me. You wore kid gloves for me. And now... you don't care. You don't care how much you hurt me."

He reminded me that he was sick. He didn't have the energy to be kind. But, he managed a weak apology all the same.

Your daddy and I left that bedroom for the sanctuary of the basement, and I collapsed with my hands over my belly. I kept thinking about the night before. It had been so perfect; Dad had been safe in the hospital, and for the first night since our trip after grandma had died, I'd slept the whole night through, curled with your daddy and the dogs. Now, here we were again, trapped in hell, and I had no idea what to do or how to breathe.

I'd like to tell you that was enough for me to leave. But you know it wasn't.

Fifteen

On a random fall mid-morning, you and I were sitting on the couch, watching something inappropriate, and your daddy was typing away at the dining room table. I'd been chewing on an idea all morning and finally found the nerve to say something. I turned to him and waited for him to notice me.

"I was thinking," I began slowly, "that I might want to go to the library. There's one close by, isn't there?"

He nodded. "When you feel a little better, you could walk there," he said. "It's literally down the road and around a corner."

I paused. It felt like such a big ask. I could feel the anxiety building in my shoulders. "Do you... do you think you could keep Boychild while I went?"

"Today?" You stopped typing and turned to look at me with that examining gaze of yours. I felt the weight of your full focus and fought the urge to cry.

"Well, I mean, it doesn't have to be today I suppose. I just... I haven't done hardly any driving and it makes me kind of nervous still and I don't really want to drive with him in the car yet and I've never been there and I just ..." my voice trailed off and I shifted you from one arm to the next nervously.

He smiled at me. "Babe. It's fine. I have a meeting in an hour, but after that, sure."

"Oh. Really? I'm going to the library today?" I might as well have been saying I'm going for an afternoon at a luxury spa. I couldn't believe the words were mine.

"Sounds like," he said.

"Huh." It's the only response I could think of. My whole body buzzed. I was suddenly the kind of person who could just decide, on a whim, to go to the library? Really? Truly, I didn't believe him - I thought for sure his meeting would run longer, or the sky would start bleeding, or something else horrific would get in the way - but, just as he promised, his meeting ended after an hour, he took you into his arms, and I... just left.

During the short drive, I struggled to remember that there was a time when I just left the house all the fucking time. Then, I realized that wasn't exactly true. For the last five years, while Dad had been sick, I always had to at least check to see if he needed something first, and he always did. Additionally, for the first three years of that, and for nearly the entire decade prior, I was responsible for Grandma. And she, for the majority of that time, could not be left alone.

So, tragically, this forty minute journey in and out of the local library was my first little taste of quiet freedom in an incredibly long time. I fought back tears as I pulled into the parking lot and held that truth close.

The smell - that sweet decaying smell of old paper and generic cleaner - wrapped around me as soon as the door swung open. It was comforting, and soft, like getting wrapped in one of Grandma's old blankets. It was a much smaller library than mine, but I didn't care. Then, I remembered: *No*. This *is mine now*.

I must have looked lost because a kid who was entirely too young for his facial hair came over with a friendly smile and a clipboard. He helped me sign up for a card and showed me around. "Oh," he said, "and don't forget you can use your card to access everything in the state system online."

It was the most exciting thing I'd heard in months.

When I got home, you were in your daddy's arms and he was walking back and forth, on the phone. I could tell it was work and felt a rush of guilt fall over me. I set down the books and reached out for you, but he waved me away and started winding down the conversation.

I told him about my discovery, and he immediately downloaded the app onto my phone. He logged me in and there it was - the entire library - at my fingertips.

I know we give technology a lot of shit, but this was amazing. For once, I was actually looking forward to your afternoon nap; while you slept on me, I wouldn't have to search for something to watch or scroll through Reddit for the millionth time. Instead, I could log on and find something decent to read.

I was looking forward to something.
I'd forgotten that was possible.

dear heart

I am
fine
    ding
my way
back
to
you

My shrink nearly danced with glee when I told
her, and she reminded me to read whatever I
wanted. It made me think of Grandma; that
woman would cut through a murder mystery or
shitty romance novel like a warm knife through
butter, and she reveled in their terribleness. She
would not be shamed for her delights, and I did
my best to follow in her footsteps.

That afternoon, after twenty minutes of
rocking and singing Rocky Racoon, I settled into
the couch with you, opened up my new app, and
disappeared into it for a full two hours.

"You know," your daddy told me a week or so
later, "you don't have to watch that video on your
phone."

I was watching Sir Ken Robinson's Ted Talk.
I'd found it years ago, looking for something to

show my students about creativity, and I gravitated back to it from time to time. There's something about his sly smile and easy humor that soothes me. Today, it was background while I repotted a pretty little ponytail palm I'd splurged on during my outing for the week.

It felt nearly sinful to have dirt under my nails again. You watched on from your bouncer, equally delighted with a dangling sheep we'd recently found.

"The new television is smart, remember? You can go straight to youtube." he said.

With a few clicks, he'd brought the same video up on the big screen. "Check it out, bug," I called to you. "We're fancy!"

It was a shift. A quiet one, like when you open the window into a stale, unused room. The air doesn't crackle with change, but it changes all the same as new life slowly wafts in. For the first time since you were born, I had something I wanted to talk about. A reason to reach out. "I just saw a video that reminded me of you," I'd text, or "weren't you telling me you were getting into photography? I just saw this beautiful book."

Sure, everyone wanted to ask how I was and talk about you. But I didn't. I didn't want to minimize or side step questions about my sanity, but I also didn't want to tell the truth.

update

I still have
nightmares
during the day. they turn me
to shadow. It's odd
he doesn't
fall
through
my fingers.

And you? You were a sentient potato. Infants
might be cute enough, and you were adorable,
but as a demographic, they are remarkably
uninteresting. I'm sorry. It's true. I just was not
under the spell that hits so many parents; I did
not find you fascinating just because you were
mine. And no one needed to hear the truth about
that either:

lately

I feel as if
I've grown
an adorable tumor

But now... now I had something to say. I
became a consumer of knowledge. Books and
videos, then documentaries and podcasts. We
were learning all day long. I remember one

particularly sweet book about trees. The idea
that trees worked together to share resources, to
prop one another up, was one that still moves
me.

waiting

the baby
cricket hops - frantic, haphazard steps -
desperate to escape
my hands.
no larger than two grains of rice, but
I can see
his antenna searching wild
for safety. "It's ok," i whisper. "I've got you."
I let him loose outside.
If I believed in a god, I'd be tempted to hope
this (this neverending stream of screaming
and nights) is just me,
scooped up in His hands,
and before too long, I'll be
dropped down to
safety.

Sixteen

I'd always considered myself a devout introvert, but now, in addition to information, I craved people. I craved noise. The only problem was that I couldn't stand to go anywhere. We tried it once; when you were first born, a friend held a welcoming party. The moment you were locked in the car, I felt a surge of panic. Everything was too suddenly loud, too bright, too much.

It was overwhelming, like nothing else I'd ever felt, and I went entirely silent. When your daddy asked if I was a bit nervous, I nodded, but I didn't elaborate. Normally, my panic attacks present with shaking and tears, but this time I just… emptied. By the time we'd reached our friends, I had disassociated completely. I've seen the pictures dozens of times, but I don't remember much of being there. What little memories I have are distorted, like I was looking up at my life from the bottom of a well.

After that, your daddy asked our friends to come to us instead.

At first, it was just one or two. We'd chat quietly and laugh about how weird and mundane parenting life had become. We stuck to safe topics, and I asked what life was like beyond my four walls. After a few afternoons of this, when I was sure I wouldn't have some sort of

breakdown and scare everyone in the room, I
encouraged your daddy to have a board game
night. Then, DND.

I had no desire to play either, but it was
another step back to normal. A normal that was,
somehow, slowly, becoming better than before.

there is laughter

in my house.
a great roar of joy comes rolling from the
livingroom.
and even though I'm tucked in bed with you, I
can
    see your daddy - the heart
    of it all. there is a pause,
    glasses clink,
    then another wave.
    it mingles with your delicate snore.

Just before your fourth month, a pair of
friends asked us out to dinner, and I surprised
everyone by saying yes. Another couple we knew
agreed to watch you, and I spent the day
oscillating between feeling it was no big deal at
all and wanting to vomit.

When the time came, I noticed - and was
surprised to find - that I didn't entirely like giving
you to someone else. I wasn't anxious, or nervous
exactly. It was just... uncomfortable. I was
acutely aware of an emptiness in my arms. *But,*

surely, I thought, *the upside to a lack of maternal bonding should be an ability to leave the fucking house, right?* I'd heard so many stories of women, paralyzed with fears, unable to leave their children alone for a few hours. There was no way that could be me. So, I pushed my discomfort aside and off we went.

Dinner itself was pleasant enough. Good food, good company, easy conversation. But I remember thinking that it was a truly stupid thing to be eating dinner at seven thirty at night. Who eats dinner that late? What were we, European? I was starting to seriously see the wisdom in an Early Bird Special and drank enough coffee to make the waitress nervous. I was yawning, my hips hurt, and I just wanted to take off my damn bra. I felt like I'd skipped motherhood entirely and gone straight to grandparent.

By the time we parted ways, I was beyond exhausted. But I had done the thing.

When we got home, your babysitters were proud to say that they had, after a tiring evening of their own, managed to get you to sleep in the crib. They left, and your daddy and I just stood there, enjoying the silence and dark.

Then, you screamed.

It was a different sound than either of us had heard before. High pitched. Keening. Your daddy went to you, and I heard him coo, trying to soothe you.

My whole body filled with a knowing. I can't
explain it any other way. "He's afraid," I called.
"He needs the light."

"I'll try to get him back down," he called back.

"No." I was strong. Decisive. I walked up to the
crib and picked up your still thrashing body.

"They got you to sleep," I whispered, "but they
left you all alone in a dark room with the door
closed." I padded out to the living room and
turned the lights down low.

"It's so awful to be scared, isn't it?" I cuddled
you close and motioned for your daddy to get a
bottle. "Yes," I answered. "It's an awful big feeling
for such a little bug. But you're safe now. You are
safe and warm and loved. And everything is
going to be okay."

Seventeen

Almost twenty years ago, when your daddy
and I were dating, we said we wanted a whole
brood of children. Five didn't seem unreasonable
at all (if we could afford it, of course), and as
many pets as we could, and we'd live in a big, but
cozy, house with ridiculous art and a mess in
every room.

someday

I dream of little toes
digging into dirt, of pants
covered in grass stains and sun.
there are dogs barking
and hens clucking
and goats doing
whatever the hell it is
that they do.
the air is filled with
cinnamon and hayseed.

We were so young.
And yet... by the time we were married, we
seemed well on our way to the kind of wildly
noisy and loving home I always dreamt of. We
were moving into a house with Dad, we already

had my cat, and there was talk of dogs and babies in the not so distant future.

It just so happened that our first baby came along in the shape of my then 83 yr old grandmother.

Shortly after our honeymoon, she had an accident. In true Marguerite fashion, she'd climbed up onto a rickety-ass chair to try and dust the top of her refrigerator. It didn't matter that she had blood pressure issues, diabetes, or that she got light headed easily. Dust would not stand in her house. Consequences be damned.

Then, she fell.

Score one for the dust.

Thankfully, she was mostly fine. But, with a nasty bump on the head and a hip that had very nearly popped out of socket, the hospital gave her a wheelchair and she came to stay with us and Dad. Temporarily, of course.

Unfortunately, shortly after she settled into the guest room, we found out that her fierce independence was getting the better of her. It was harder to get on and off the bus with groceries, so on the weeks I didn't shop for her, she was living on cheerios and instant coffee. It was harder to remember to balance her bank, and her credit card bills were piling up. She didn't feel like socializing most days, so she hadn't noticed she needed a hearing aid. And because she needed one, she admitted she often felt scared at the doctor's because she didn't understand.

"She should come live with us permanently," I said. I was talking to Dad about it in the kitchen while she napped. Your daddy was at work.

"I know you love your grandmother," he said, "but I don't want her here. You know we don't get along. She drives me crazy. I... I don't want to feel that way in my own home."

We agreed to try to find her a facility that was close enough for me to visit every week, and we agreed to wait to talk to her about it until we had more information. Unfortunately for my father, grandma made less than nine hundred dollars a month through social security and any savings she had was long gone. There was no way we could afford anything that I would trust. Unfortunately for me, Grandma was as stubborn as I was.

"Sweetie," she said, "I love you. But I live alone. I have lived alone for over twenty years now, and it's staying that way."

I decided to do what I could with the time that I had. Her cognition got better after eating more nutritiously, and I squared away her creditors. I talked to her about delivering groceries once a week instead of every few, and bringing up some bulk stuff once a month. We bought her some newer clothes, and some more secure shoes, and I taught her to use a cane.

At the end of three months, her doctor declared her healed. So, I asked her one last time if she was sure she wanted to leave. She was adamant. That weekend, we packed the car up and your daddy and I prepared to drive her back home. As she was coming down the stairs, she broke down into tears. "I don't want to go back home," she whimpered. "I don't want to go back."

I grabbed her into a hug. "You're not going anywhere. This is your home."

Sometimes, I think that's the moment - long before his illness - when Dad decided it was okay to hate me.

When she had calmed down, we got her back upstairs. I started making plans to get her things and let HUD know she didn't need her place anymore. At some point, Dad pulled me aside. "If she lives here," he said, "she's your responsibility. I'll pay for appointments and things, but I'm not taking care of her."

And just like that, I was a grad student, a retail worker, and a full time caregiver.

She was my perpetual tween: independent enough to use the microwave and entertain herself and take a shower, but dependent on me for everything else. My entire life had a new layer to it.

I feel I should note, for the sake of fairness, that Dad had a point. She was a complete shit as a mother and, when in the right mood, would admit as much. But, she loved me. Without condition. She was the only one who ever had. I was her grandbaby. I was perfect. And we trusted each other. Always. It was the first time I had ever actively gone against my father's wishes, and I have no regrets.

She was, in many ways, the mom I always needed. Her advice was always dated, and more than a little sexist, but she listened earnestly whenever I talked about work or my relationships. She helped me pick out clothes, and teased me when my hair was shorter than she'd like, and reminded me, every day, that she was proud of who I was.

Just as much as she was my replacement mother, I was her second chance child. Her own daughter had financially, emotionally, and physically abused her to the point where I intercepted all phone calls. She was the reason Marguerite had no savings. The reason she quivered whenever an unknown number appeared on the phone. So, I reminded her what it was to be loved, too.

She lived with us for the next twelve years. Taking care of her wove itself into my life. Instead of pursuing full time work, I started adjunct teaching so I could be back before she ever woke up. Instead of vacations, your daddy and I took day trips and staycations. And, instead of children, we got dogs. Still, every year was a little harder. A few more pills, a few more things she couldn't do, a few more incontinence episodes or diabetic coma near misses. And then, after just over a month with hospice, she was gone.

She died in our living room. A few days prior, I'd watched her slip into a coma, fighting just long enough to grab my hand and push out an "I love you." Now, I was standing beside her bed, watching her breathe. I started to walk towards the kitchen, but something caught my eye, and I

turned back around just to see her body settle. I
waited for the next breath in, but it never came.

"I think she's dead," I whispered. Your daddy
came from the kitchen and agreed. I don't know
how long we stood there, watching her not be.

this stings

my heart
is full

of bees.

I had promised Grandma that we would have a
baby once she died. She understood that caring
for her, plus a newborn, was too much to ask, and
she'd resigned herself to never knowing you, but
she knew we wanted kids. "You will be such a
good mother," she told me. She said it whenever I
fixed something small for her: lunch, untangled a
necklace, reached something high off a shelf.
Even now, if I close my eyes and really listen, I
can hear her: "you will be such a good mother."

We decided to wait a year to start trying. My
IUD would need to come out then anyway, and I
wanted to take some time. I wanted to breathe,
and to grieve, to spend some time taking care of
myself now that I was no longer taking care of
her and before I was taking care of you. I wanted
to remember what it was like to be a person, not
a caregiver.

I never really got the chance, though. Not even a month after she died, our older dog fell terribly ill. The vet doesn't really know what happened, but something kicked off liver failure and within a week, he was dead.

It was sad, of course. He was a good boy and a sweet boy and a good older brother for our new puppy. But, truthfully, I felt the same kind of sad relief that I had when Grandma died. This pup had skin issues and eye issues and allergy issues and breathing issues and even needed me to wipe his ass after most poops. For eight years, I kept him alive with vet trips and special food and medications and supplements and anything else I could try.

Still, dad had always considered him *his* dog, and he mourned accordingly. Up until this point, as his illness had intensified, he'd become increasingly unwilling to do anything for himself; he was too tired to fix himself breakfast, he'd say, too sore to clean his bathroom, too fuzzy to put his clothes away or make his doctors appointments. He'd even stopped brushing his teeth.

I knew these were classic depression symptoms, and watched as they built with a slow intensity. Before our dog's death, I did my best to take care of everything but the teeth and tried not to think about the fact that he was finding energy to talk to my brother's friends about marijuana cookie recipes or empty his closets, leaving bags of things for me to deal with, because he was "sick of dressing like an old man."

I tried to give him grace because, after all, he was sick. And, I figured, even if he had hated her, somewhere he might be missing Marguerite, and that was making things worse, too.

By the time our dog died, the only thing I could convince Dad to do with any kind of regularity was to come downstairs for an hour or so while I cleaned his room.

Now?

He stayed firmly in his makeshift recliner. He spent hours telling the same stories, going over old photos and videos. Everything reminded him of his pup and the smallest reminder would send him into an hour long tear-filled rant about how his baby was taken too young, the doctors were all idiots, and he'd never trusted that vet even though I'd been taking our other animals there for years.

I would remind him that he shouldn't eat something or he needed to do his physical therapy and be met with screaming; "I'm fucking sad," he'd roar. " I just lost my best friend. He was the only one who understood me and now he's gone. I am going to eat what the fuck I want. Okay?" Or I'd tell him I couldn't sit with him any longer because I needed to go to work or the grocery store. "Oh sure," he'd scoff, "I know you're sick of me. It's not my fault I'm *sad*, you know. None of this is my fault."

I empathized for him. I did. After all, I was grieving too. Every day, I was brought face to face with some reminder that Grandma was gone: a scarf she'd knitted fell from the top of a closet, her perfume bottle peeked out from behind a pile of towels. But any time I tried to bring her up, even in the context of how much she, too, loved that damned dog, he'd snap at me for not being willing to sit with *his grief.* He didn't seem to miss her at all and was clearly offended that I did.

The whole thing hit harder than it might have because his grief over our dog triggered memories of the last pet I'd lost, and I suddenly saw it all in a new, terrible light. Just a few years prior, I had to put down my 15 yr old cat. I tell people it's because he scratched Grandma and started biting, but the truth is that our new hyperactive 12 week old puppy - our now dead dog - terrorized him to insanity, and I was not strong enough to stop it.

Much to Dad's dismay, I tried to put up gates and create safe spaces, but, much like with Zero, the dog kept getting in. I watched my shelter kitten, already neurotic and twitchy from his first year of life as a stray, devolve into a terrified mess of a creature. When he did bite Grandma, I asked the vet what to do; they told me aggressive animals rarely get adopted out, let alone aggressive elderly animals. So, after 14 years together, I put him out of his misery.

When it happened, I had been forced to do my crying and reminiscing with your daddy or alone. Dad would have none of it. Unlike his current dog, mine had been "just an asshole cat." Besides, he'd remind, I still had the puppy to dote over if I wanted a fur-covered hug. "After all," he had dismissed, sick of my moping demeanor "animals die all the time."

I couldn't help but wonder just how violent he'd get now if I was brave enough to tell him the same.

Eighteen

I don't remember much of the holiday season after Grandma died. I know we still bought gifts, and I still made cookies and decorated the house, but I don't remember that sad nostalgia I always feel putting everything away. Mostly, I just kept moving through the motions because I knew she'd hate it if she ruined my holidays. She never wanted me to feel sad. "I'm old," she used to say, long before she was sick. She'd shrug her shoulders and sort of wave her hands in the air, flippant. "All my friends are dead already. Just... I dunno, sweetie. Just screw it and move on."

After the holidays, though, I decided it was time to stop.

I'd taken a sabbatical from teaching over the fall, and I decided to take the spring off as well. With Grandma gone, I wasn't even sure I wanted to adjunct anymore. Besides, this was right when Dad's health started getting exponentially worse. He started having bouts of insomnia, long stretches of pain in his hips or chest, and the list of foods he refused to eat just kept growing.

In retrospect, it all makes sense. Of course his hips hurt; now that he was in mourning for his dog, he only ever got out of his chair to go to the bathroom. Of course he had insomnia; his vitamin D levels were through the floor because he refused to let me open the curtains or come get some sun on the deck. Of course he was obsessed with food; between the opioids and pot, he was always either nauseated or starving. Of course his pain would swell just large enough to take what little time I'd carved away for myself; that's what narcissists do.

But, I didn't see any of that at the time. I only saw someone I loved in pain and knew it was my job to somehow fix it. I kept thinking if only, if only, if only. If only I could cook the right thing. If only I could get him to sleep. If only I could find him someone to talk to, or get my brother over to play chess with him, or convince him to start coming downstairs again. Then, maybe, I could break this spell and he'd go back to being, at least occasionally, kind.

But nothing was enough to break through, and, every day, I tried a little harder. By the spring before my pregnancy, I was taking up all of his meals, sorting his meds, cleaning his room, and paying his bills. By this point, marijuana had been legalized in our state, so I could get him out of the house to hit up the local dispensary from time to time. But that was it. I still held out hope, though, that I could help him push to the other side of his depression. I was so delusionally optimistic; so I spent hours in his room with him to help stave off his self-induced loneliness. Sometimes, we would talk about books or philosophy like when I was younger. Mostly, though, we watched the news and he theorized about why my generation was ruining everything.

Once, I made the mistake of telling him about a book on race I'd been reading. He went on a twenty minute tirade about how white people who grew up poor and marginalized couldn't possibly be racist. I doubled down on my "mistake" by trying to explain that, at least as far as the book explained, it didn't work that way. I was informed I was "everything that's wrong with this country," and then subjected to another hour of "libertarian" news.

You'd think that he'd want to spend as little time with me as possible, given how stupid he seemed to think I was. But the opposite was true. I'd stopped going to the gym, or grocery store, or anywhere really because every time I told him I was leaving, he would berate me for running away. When I started gaining weight, he started taunting me that I sat on my ass all day. But the moment I took up walking, or started talking about going for a bike ride, he'd whine about how "nice it must be to get outside. You never take me anywhere. I'd love to go for a walk sometime." And then, when I'd offer to help him join, I was ridiculous for considering what was clearly impossible.

The only thing I could leave his room to do was to spend time with your daddy.

It took me years to realize how sexist that bullshit is.

I couldn't leave to take care of my own physical and mental wellbeing, but my husband needed something? Oh, well. That was a different story.

Thank God your daddy used this for good, and would often pop into the room to say he needed me for something as a means to rescue me. We'd walk down the first flight of stairs together and he'd hold me until I stopped wanting to scream.

It never once occurred to me to leave, or that something was wrong with how I was being treated. I started having daily panic attacks again. Insomnia sprouted back up, and so did hallucinations. That's what happens when someone you love tells you that you're not worth anything every day: you start to believe.

god.

there are places in me now
that open like a cliff
into
             Nothing

But I insisted I was fine. Even to my shrink, who I'd started seeing shortly after Grandma died. I had to be fine. This time, I had to be fine. Deep in the underbelly of my mind, I thought I *couldn't be a good daughter for mom, but I can do it for dad. I'll find a way, and he'll love me again. I will love him back to whole.*

Nineteen

The year before my pregnancy wasn't all bad, though. In fact, something wonderful was happening. I was finally embracing a long-dormant truth: I am queer. I have always been so. It seems silly, I suppose, to consider that it took so long to realize, but that's one of the casualties of marrying your high school sweetheart; the opportunities for sexual discovery don't exactly abound. When you couple that with the fact that I grew up in the 90s - not exactly a bastion of tolerance and inclusivity - it becomes less surprising that I didn't figure out I am about as straight as a traffic circle until nearly five years into marriage.

Thankfully, I was lucky enough to be able to confide in your daddy and, over the years, I transitioned from bicurious to bisexual to pansexual to what I am now, which is something along the lines of I-don't-care-how-you-identify-I-think-youre-cute -and-sweet-so-lets-make-out.

For a long time, he and I had a running joke that after he died (because the husband always goes first), I'd find a nice girl to settle down with. In the meantime, I'd be the cool wife who talks about how hot actresses are and agreed to go to strip joints.

After grandma died, though, I found myself questioning the paradigm. I didn't understand why my love and commitment to your daddy meant I was going to have to ignore this whole other part of myself. By that point, I was starting to wonder about my gender identity as well, but that was too scary to say aloud to anyone: myself included. Still... if I did get brave enough to, one day, say what I was too afraid to, would it even matter? Was I going to have to ignore that too?

That's all Dad was forcing me to do, day after day, ignore my wants. My desires. Who I was. Would I really be okay if my marriage forced me to do the same?

I knew it wouldn't be, but I had no idea what I wanted to even ask for.

A divorce? No.

A threesome? Eww.

As far as I knew, there wasn't anything else. So, I sat on it.

Then, one magical afternoon at a little bookstore in the middle of nowhere, your daddy happened to pick up a copy of The Ethical Slut because he loved the name and thought it would make me laugh. Neither of us had any idea it was one of the seminal works on polyamory. I tore through it, circling and underlining like a madman. When we realized polyamory was a thing you could do, it was like an entire warehouse of light bulbs lit up above both our heads.

We've been lucky. Not all established couples survive the transition. My shrink helped a lot, and we took the time to learn what all could go wrong. We talked about it all the time, and it was a much needed distraction from the drudgery of my day. It turned out a few of our close friends were polyamorous, and they sent me lists of books and articles to read.

I'd be stuck upstairs with Dad, but instead of fighting to tune out of what he said, I'd daydream about how I was going to word my dating profile or what I was going to write for an entry in my codependency workbook while he droned on about the latest marijuana discovery or political cat fight. It was the first time in a long time I fantasized about something other than his death. Or mine.

Still, after the second or third book, I had to stare at the fact that your daddy and I had become a we. He was still a person all by himself. But me? I couldn't remember the last time I'd gone out with friends by myself, or watched a movie that I wanted even if no one else did, or spent any time by myself at all. Ever.

"That's kind of fucked up," I told your daddy. "Don't you think?"

"I do," he said. "We should fix that."

So, I did the unthinkable: I lied to Dad. I told him I was going out with your daddy, but really I was getting dropped off at a coffee shop while your daddy went to a game shop. I'd sit and read or write for an hour and then he'd pick me up and corroborate the lie when we got home. I felt like a spy, and knew damned well how sad that was.

The knowing spurred me on to push farther. I started reaching out to some very old friends and talking on the phone. I even went out to lunch with them from time to time. Dad didn't like it, but I was too excited to care. "You'll be fine," I'd tell him. "You can call if you need anything."

It was like what I had hoped for right after Grandma had died; I was finding my peace again. My place.

By the summer before my pregnancy, I was ready to date. Well, I was ready to try. Your daddy decided he would not date yet. He wanted me to take the chance to explore my sexuality without worrying about any jealousy or anxieties that might pop up.

I was still sorting through my gender in the back of my mind, and hadn't even talked to your daddy about it yet, so I decided to hold off on that for the moment. That seemed like a problem for Future Skadi to figure out. Besides, I didn't want to wait any longer. I wanted to go be a person among the people. So, I put together a profile and started swiping.

I could not believe I matched with someone. And then another someone. And then a third. Truly, I would have sooner believed a flat earther. We spent some time talking through the app, and then through text, and then, before I really believed it, I had a date with a lovely someone at a coffee house in the city.

All this time, I'd avoided telling Dad. I figured there wasn't really anything to tell until I was actively dating, so why give him a chance to shit all over everything. Your daddy offered to keep lying - to drop me off and pick me up - but that seemed unsustainable. And, more than anything, I just didn't want to. So, I told him three hours before my very first date. "I know I'm a little jittery today," I said. "The thing is... I'm bisexual, and we are polyamorous, and I'm going on a date with a woman this evening."

Tact has never been my strong suit.

Amusingly, he wasn't surprised at my sexuality announcement. Or, if he was, he hid it well. He said something along the lines of "well, now I guess I don't have to hide my porn anymore," and then dropped it.

He was, however, extremely concerned about the rest. He hollered down for your daddy and peppered him with questions: was this what he wanted? Was he really okay with this? Was I blowing up his marriage? Was he really going to let me date other people? Other men if I wanted to?

"I get that you'd want to, you know, with other women," Dad motioned, "and if she's fine with that then whatever. But really? This is ok with you?"

Even I picked up on the misogyny that time.

Your daddy confirmed that he was, in fact, okay, and I went out on my date. It wasn't terrible as far as first dates go. It was mostly meh. But it was *my* meh. The next was a little better, and the next a little better than that.

Dad still gave me crap for going out, but I found out, very quickly, that if I offered up information about who I was going to see or where we were going to go he'd get so visibly squicked out that he'd basically demand me to get out of the room. And I would. Happily.

By the end of the summer, I'd been on a handful of first dates, had made new casual and platonic friends, had chatted online with all kinds of interesting people, and had just started feeling sparks with a new special someone.

You might be wondering, little love, ... what does all this have to do with you?

It's true that when we first embarked on opening our relationship, we thought it would maybe lead to some fun stories and great sex: none of which you need to know about. However, before either of those things happened, I gained something else from dating; as I navigated relationships with brand new people, I had the chance to relearn what the fuck boundaries were and how to healthily uphold them. And only then did I see, for the first time in my thirty some years, that Dad seemed to be perfectly fine stomping all over mine. More importantly, I realized something else: I wasn't entirely sure I was okay with it.

Twenty

You are four months now, and contemplating how to knock the laundry basket over as I move clothes from washer to dryer. "Hey babe," I call over to your daddy, "Do you think I might have CPTSD? I've been reading this book, and a lot of the symptoms feel really familiar."

He turns away from his computer to look at us. "Did you think that you *didn't* have it?" He sounds almost amused.

"I mean, I didn't know it was a thing. I knew about PTSD, and I know I have that from chonker's birthapalooza, but I didn't know about the other thing. No."

"Sweetie. You zoom your therapist like once a week. How has this not come up?"

"Probably because I spend the entire hour talking about how I'm still having intrusive thoughts and wondering, pretty regularly, if I'd even care if the baby fell onto the sidewalk and died," I said, defensively, "we don't spend a lot of time talking about *my* childhood."

"But, like, the stuff with your dad *just* happened." He offered, carefully.

I sat with it for a minute and started the dryer up. You weren't laughing yet, but you clearly liked the noise.

"Was it really that bad?" I asked. "I mean, sure, he's been an asshole off and on my whole life, but he was just so sick. Right? It's not like he actually hit me or molested me or anything. He just... made me feel small and awful all the time."

I got quiet. Your daddy waited.

"Was I abused?" I asked it in the smallest voice I have. "Did he abuse me?" I tried not to let my tears plop down onto your little face. I found myself hugging you, weirdly comforted by your squirming warmth.

"I think... I think we wouldn't be having this conversation if you didn't already know the answer to that question," he responded softly.

"Well, fuck." It came out in a rush. I took a deep breath and somehow felt better. I'd named it. "How the fuck did I not see that? I mean, I knew Mom was a shit and my stepdad was a shit and, really, all of my family is a dumpster fire. But I thought Dad was..." my voice cracked and shrank. "He was a bad guy?"

It felt so stupid. I felt so stupid. I kept shoving tears away and more would come. I held you close and walked down the short hallway to sit beside him at the table.

"It would have been nice," I whimpered, "to have at least one parent who loved me."

He put his arm around me, around us, and let me cry. When you started to fuss, he took you, and I watched him. He parented so effortlessly... every action was full of love. I had always assumed I'd had a parent like that, at least a little bit, at least sometimes.

But now I wasn't so sure.

"Oh," I sighed. I took a breath and felt myself steady. "Also, I'm pretty sure I've been dissociating for years, too."

He smiled at me, but it was filled with sadness. "Yeah, babe. I know."

I looked at him. I studied the bags under his eyes, and the way his skin crinkled into wrinkles along the outermost rim of his cheeks. He was middle aged. We both were. We'd been together my entire adult life. How much of it had I spent hiding in my head? How much of it had I missed?

"Well, that's fucking ridiculous," I spat out. "He can't hurt me anymore. None of them can. Right? I'm... I'm out. I'm done. I mean, I have no idea how to get my body to actually believe me, but I figured out how to fall asleep while holding this little idiot. I'm gonna figure it out."

Anger rose up in me. I looked down at you, still in your daddy's arms, and it clicked into place: no wonder I didn't want to love you. Everyone I'd ever loved (save your daddy) had hurt me.

"Christ. Well. I guess I'm doing this again."

"What?"

Now it was my turn to smile wryly. "Bashing my head through a wall."

I didn't mean literally, though. I was referring to my own brand of exposure therapy.

Now, exposure therapy isn't for everyone. Sometimes, it's the exact wrong thing to do. But I have found, over the years, that sometimes, the only way out is through. Back when I was thirty,

I'd taken a full year to actively scare the shit out of myself as a way to get over a series of phobias. Before that, when I was seventeen, I spent a year and some change forcing panic attacks in an effort to learn to drive.

demolition

sometimes,
the only
way out
is to bash and bloody
a head through.
brick crumbles
eventually, and
concussions mostly heal.

So, I was going to do the thing that terrified me. I was going to act like I loved myself, like I was worthy of love from others, and like I was already bonded with you. And I was going to trust that, on the other side of what would feel like hell, I wouldn't have to act anymore.

ugly truths

I am not beautiful. I am -
even now after all these weeks -
covered in
purple and pockmarks.

viscera. my outsides match
my ins.

I started staring at myself in the mirror. I'd
been doing some minor exercise and yoga for
about a month, but my body still carried the
marks, and weight, of pregnancy. Even though I
hated the aftereffects, I was weirdly proud of
myself for gaining weight during pregnancy. That
might seem like a strange thing to say - being
proud of gaining a hundred pounds - but both my
parents were fatphobic to their cores. Yet, I had
managed to push their voices outside of my head
for a whole nine months. *You are 3D printing a
person*, I had told myself. I was going to eat
whatever the hell I wanted.
Now, though, those voices were back in full
force. Every time I saw my reflection, they were
in my ear.

mirror mirror

I keep the scale in the closet.
I know what it would say:
    I'm fat.
The mirror agrees,
but clarifies: not In the acceptable way.

This was certainly the heaviest I've ever been,
but I've always been on the thicker end of fit.

When I was your age, and for all of elementary
school, I greeted the world belly first. I don't
remember Mom ever saying anything to me
directly; she never explicitly put me on a diet, or
had me counting my calories, but she made sure I
knew the difference between good and bad foods
from an early age.

Chicken breast? Good. Salad dressing? Bad. My
snacking options were always either fat free,
sugar free, or both. The one treat I was allowed
was a small bowl of regular ice cream. I'd eat it
every night in the kitchen with Mom while she
ate a bowl of fat free.

My first memory of getting outright shamed
for my body came when I was eight. We were at
the doctor's office, and I hopped up onto one of
those scales with the measuring stick attached. I
stood as straight as I could, wondering if I'd
gotten any taller. I remembered the doctor
tinkered with the scale, then chuckled. "I guess I
don't have to ask if she's having any trouble
eating," he said.

Even though I was wearing a fabric gown with
little bears on it, I felt naked and struggled not to
squirm from the flush of shame that settled over
me. My mother shook her head and smiled, "no.
That's never a problem with her."

That night, she switched my ice cream to hers.

At first glance, Dad seemed to be the
opposite. He was fat for most of my childhood,
and he went out of his way to encourage us to eat
whatever we wanted. A regular Friday night was

an entire extra large pizza per child plus a pint of ice cream each. A firm member of the Clean Plate Club, he would celebrate as we finished the last of it; "such healthy appetites," he'd applaud. I used to think this was just his way of counteracting Mom's diet insanity. Now I understand it's more likely that he just wanted company and validation while engaging in his own weekly binge.

Attitudes towards us aside, though, I have always known that Dad hated the way he looked; I don't remember not knowing this. He'd been fit right up until his divorce with Mom, and he'd routinely reminisce about how fast he used to run or how often he practiced martial arts. He'd constantly tell us how important it was to have some sort of exercise regime because we didn't want to end up like him when we were older.

But, I loved that Dad was fat. For one, it made me feel less embarrassed about my own baby-fat belly. It was more than that, though. His size was incredibly comforting. He's a tall man, and between that and the weight, it was like walking next to a mountain. Yes, it was terrifying when he yelled or stomped around the apartment. But when he held my hand to cross the street, or when he made himself taller as he spoke to my stepdad, I felt protected by the most powerful force on Earth.

He did diet, from time to time, but not in the same consistent way Mom did. Instead, he focused on exercise. He'd buy gadgets, equipment, and gym memberships determined to sweat off the weight. In his eyes, the one bright spot of his current illness was that he managed to lose over a hundred pounds in a little less than a year. "Look at me," he'd tell me, just a few months before I left, "I'm thin again!"

Of course, he was too frail to stand for more than ten minutes, still refused to leave his chair, and, by that time, had attraphied to the point of needing hip surgery. It didn't stop him from openly planning to start running again, though. "Now that I'm so thin, my ankles won't hurt anymore," he'd say. "I can start once all the ice is off the ground."

By then, I knew better; he was never going to go running again. But I smiled and oohed when he bought new shoes. After his surgery, I'd listen to him tell his temporary physio therapist all about his plans while simultaneously dodging questions about his eating habits. In his mind, Exercise will always be King.

To wit, I absolutely believe the proudest my father has ever been of me was when I was fourteen and taking a kickboxing class after school. I was practicing my form in our living room when he called my brother over. "See that? Look at those amazing calf muscles," he beamed. "That's what hard work looks like."

Since then, I have achieved a master's degree, a successful marriage, a darling son, and my fair share of awards and accolades in my various professions. He has never as spoken as warmly of me as he did back then.

When I was a teenager, I'd hoped that one of the few benefits of leaving Mom's was that I could eat whatever I wanted, like had Dad let me do on the weekends. It was the slimmest of silver linings. But, somehow, Dad seamlessly took on policing my food for her. When I was vegan, I ate too little protein. When I was Atkins, I ate too little fiber. When I was gluten free, I was a pain on the ass. When I was on my period, and ate whatever I wanted, I was giving in and not thinking about my long-term goals.

"You don't want to be like me, do you?" He'd ask.

***

Now, four months after having you, I weighed as much as he had back then. *Just one more thing about me for him to hate*, I thought, ruefully.

I stared at myself in the mirror. I felt his hate, and my mother's disgust, well up inside me. So much of my body had changed. Did I even know how my pieces fit together anymore? I closed my eyes and tried to feel... me. But everything felt out of alignment, structurally unsound, and just... wrong.

"You have been through so much, haven't you," I whispered. The compassion in my voice caught me off guard, and I started to tear up. I couldn't find any hate, disgust, or contempt anymore. I was just sad. And overwhelmed. I wanted to reach out and give that stranger in the mirror a hug.

downward dog

from your rocker,
you watch me
raise these broken hips
as high as they will
go. i hold,
feeling
the blood pull loose,
feeling
the breath open
feeling
everything sigh.

I shift and push forward to plank.

just long enough
to kiss you "hello."

Twenty-One

You got a big kick out of my new daily yoga. I would watch your face light up as I peekabooed you when my face came back up from downward dog or back down from cobra. I set your bouncer up so that I could place a foot on either side and talk to you from warrior one, two, or three. I would lay my head at your feet for the pigeon pose, feel my hips and lower back, and try to breathe.

After two weeks, I started to rise out of the last pose and an audible pop rippled through my left leg. At first, I wasn't sure what had happened. My whole leg tingled, like a limb coming back from sleep. Then I noticed; it didn't hurt to stand up. I'd dislocated my hip during your birth, and it had still hurt; I didn't have full range of motion, and something pinched with every step.

Only, now it didn't.

It felt like a sign from the universe that I was finally headed in the right direction. A pat on the back from an invisible hand. Emboldened by the victory, I screwed up the nerve to ask your daddy for a favor.

"I want a shower," I said. I was irritated at how insecure I felt. I'd just made a damn person. But my voice shook with near-tears.

"Now?"

"No. I mean. Well, yeah. That would be nice. But I mean every day. Before you start work, or before you go to work, I want twenty minutes for a shower and to eat without a baby on my lap." I wiped away a tear.

"Why are you crying?"

"Because I'm afraid you'll say no," I whimpered, feeling ridiculous.

"Babe. You just made a person. I'm pretty sure we can get you a shower every day."

"That's what I'm saying!" I shouted it, startling you. You looked up at me with your first real what-the-fuck face, and I started laughing. You just kept staring at me, and the idea that this small, constantly needy, sentient potato of a person dared to be irritated at me, the person literally keeping it alive, was hysterical.

"Babe? You ok over there?"

I tried to explain, but it came out in fits and bursts, and he started chuckling at me.

I laughed hard enough that tears came down my face and I needed to sit down. I laughed so hard I peed myself. Then, I took a gloriously long shower.

finding myself

last night,
I dreamt I was covered in sequins and jewels
from the dollar store. I was
singing, off key and loud,
with women I didn't know, and

we laughed until
I woke up
covered in your pee

A few days later, I found the courage to take you to the doctor for the first time. You'd actually been sleeping well, and I felt the closest to rested since checking into the hospital. Your daddy strapped you into the carseat, and I carried you in it to the car. It felt heavy and uneven in my hands, and I was shaky with nerves. I must have checked the directions half a dozen times even though your daddy just plugged it into the GPS for me.

While I listened to the car seat click into place, I took a few purposeful breaths. I felt my hips groan and my lower back tighten as my fragile body worked to conform to the seat. I realized it was the first time I'd been in a car in weeks and, for a moment, wondered how long it took before someone forgot how to drive.

Your daddy closed your door; then, as if he'd read my mind, he reached in to hug me and whispered, "you'll be fine." He kissed me on the forehead and closed my door for me. "You've got this," he mouthed from the other side of the window.

"All right, little bit," I said. I watched you in the mirror. "Let's go do this."

The moment I put my foot to the gas, my anxiety dissipated. The drive was hardly ten minutes long, but the whole time I felt... normal.

Easy. Good, even. I pulled into the parking lot and, concerned I'd never figure out how to jam that stupid carseat back into place, unstrapped you and carried you in.

The receptionist smiled at me while we waited. You were fascinated with the reflections on the window behind me and the way the light danced on the road outside. I narrated what you saw; "there are so many cars today," I said softly, "green and black and a white truck. How exciting." You gurgled back from my arms, content.

They called us back, and I caught a glimpse of us in the hallway mirror. Immediately, I was pulled out of the good mood I'd been slowly cultivating. The woman in the mirror was an enormous stranger. She walked slowly, almost painfully. It stung to see; I might have been feeling a bit better on the inside over the last few days and weeks, but from the outside? I was the same old trainwreck, and it was devastating to know that was the only thing people could see.

As we walked down the hall, the mirror followed us, and I tried to focus on you instead of me. But, that was just as jarring. How the hell were you so small? The whole hospital had classified you as "the big baby" when you were born, and you had been steadily growing, I knew.

You were this larger than life presence every single day. So how was it that now, looking in this mirror, all I saw was a fragile, tiny, impossibly vulnerable speck of a human being? I found myself hugging you tighter, hoping you weren't too cold.

The visit itself was uneventful. The doctor was uninterested, but kind, and if she thought I was crazy, she'd decided it wasn't problematically so. She offered an information sheet on developmental milestones, then left while we waited for the nurse.

field trip

after the vaccines,
you scream into me with all
the fury your smallness
can muster.
"I've got you,"
I whisper:
"I'm your momma
and I've got you."
you settle.
it's the first time I say this truth out loud.

Twenty-Two

The summer before I got pregnant was a hopeful one. After a nearly never ending winter of grief, it seemed like life was finally starting to bloom again.

I was dating, which was wild, and I laughed with your daddy over ridiculous first date stories and second date butterflies. Even though I wasn't quite clicking with any special someones, it was joyous to be out of the house. Out in the world. Out of Dad's room. For the first time in years, I wasn't just a caregiver anymore. I was a person again.

We were making headway with Dad's illness, too. I'd managed to get him to follow a diet protocol long enough for them to finally agree to test him for something new. Miraculously, they'd discovered an issue with his throat, and he was a good candidate for a low-risk surgery. Before the surgery, they tested his blood and found one of his vitamins was severely deficient, and that the most prevalent side effect of this was pain and mood swings. Now, he could take supplements.

I kept thinking that he'd finally come out of his darkness and remember that he loved me. It was just the illness, I thought. He was just in pain.

Our family doctor, delighted at the prospect of an upcoming surgery, convinced him to try an ssri to help him prepare. We'd talked on the phone, her and I, many times about his depression. Now, it seemed, she had finally found a reasonable excuse for him; "you've been chronically ill for so long," she said, "of course you are depressed. You take this now, then the depression won't follow you after your surgery."

I know that's not exactly how it works, but I didn't fully care. As far as I was concerned, we were finally in real business. Sure, he had sleeping pills and xanax and medical marijuana, but he refused to use them as intended; he'd go a few days without them, then take a day and decide to numb out by doubling up on everything. Once numb, he'd decide to stay numb, and sort of hover in a drug induced meanness for anywhere between a week to a couple days.

He wouldn't be able to do that with an ssri, though. It's totally different. After all, my own ssri had been life altering: I used to have multiple panic attacks a day and spent the rest of my time ebbing in and out of depression. Lexapro, which I'd been on for about a year at that point, gave my system a chance to pause and breathe.

And that's all Dad needs, I thought, *a break.* Then, he wouldn't want to just numb out all the time. He'd start coming downstairs. He'd start trying again. He'd go back to being Dad.

While we waited for his surgery, I started a new job working as a medical receptionist, and it was strangely wonderful. For 20 hours a week, I sat at a desk and chatted with patients and kept the office organized. I even started running on my lunch break. Dad was always a little fussy when I got home, but I would take him breakfast before I left and leave him lunch in a cooler.

He never really wanted to hear about my day, but I'd tell him anyway. From the beginning, he'd comment on how he'd rather I just stayed at home - wasn't I going to stay home when I started having kids anyway? - but I'd brush him off, reminding him that his savings was dwindling, and I didn't want us to have to rely on it anymore.

It was a valid concern on my part, considering that, for quite a while now Dad had basically been paying me to take care of him. I didn't get a paycheck or anything, and your daddy's salary was just barely covering all of my actual bills, but Dad was where I went for any miscellaneous expenditures: new clothes, eating out money, etc. At the time, it all seemed easy enough; I'd ask him when I wanted something, and he'd buy it for me. Or not.

It wasn't until I had my own money again that I realized how infantilizing it had been. I hadn't even been given the autonomy of an allowance; I'd been like a little kid, having to beg after every purchase that I wanted. For someone who preached feminism and equality, I couldn't help but notice that he'd been pretty damn happy to treat my fiances as if I were a 1950s housewife. And, a mistrustred one at that.

But now, I *did* have my own money again, and it was glorious. I didn't have to ask for money to go to the movies, or to buy a book, or for anything at all. I wasn't rich, of course, but I was making enough to be able to start going out on the weekends with your daddy. We'd been two broke college students for so long, we'd almost forgotten what it was like to walk up to the local deli for a cup of coffee and order more than just stale croissants.

After a few weeks of this, I noticed Dad was upping his medication again. Once he'd received an actual diagnosis, with a surgery on the horizon, he'd stopped double-dosing and numbing out for the most part. But, now, he was at it again. Instead of a xanax or an edible, he was combining them. Instead of taking two sleeping pills at night, he was sometimes taking one first thing in the morning. And, often, with another edible.

He's just in pain, I told myself.

I figured he was lonely, too, and still battling depression, but nothing I did had any effect. We tinkered with his ssri, and that did improve things at first. But, it was short lived. Then, it was just like in the beginning: every time I offered to do something for him that I thought he might enjoy, or offered to arrange to have my brother come over for a visit, or offered to have him see whatever kind of professional he was comfortable with, I managed to always get it wrong.

No matter what I suggested, it always wound around to him yelling at me and nearly always culminated in him telling me to just "go away since I'm such a burden."

The only real upside to all of this double-dosing was that it led to him sleeping a lot of the time, and the only time I wasn't doing something wrong was when he was asleep. So, I called the doctor to make sure he wasn't in any medical danger at mixing substances and then forced myself to let it go.

He's just in pain.

My therapist was helping me build boundaries for dating, and they bled over to my relationship with Dad during the weekends. I asked that we stop watching so much news, and I put a table in his room so I could keep myself busy crafting.

I would tell him I was going to only spend an hour or two with him, and then, despite his cajoling, I would leave when I said. And when he decided to try smoking again, and starting trying to hotbox me again, I would ignore his protests and open the windows.

Finally, on those days when the only thing that seemed to bring a smile to Dad's face was making me feel small, I stopped going upstairs at all; I'd send your daddy in with his food instead.

Making boundaries is hard, though. At the time, enforcing any boundary at all - no matter how small - felt a little like stabbing someone you love with an icepick over something like they rolled the toilet paper the wrong way. Even now, after years of therapy, it often feels like an overreaction to something I shouldn't be reacting to at all.

To assuage my guilt at standing up for myself (and yes, I understand how ridiculous that is) I tried to have your daddy spend time with us upstairs, so that I could spend more time with Dad but still have your daddy in the room as a buffer. We both knew Dad would be at least civil with him in the room.

We got to watching a few shows together and would sometimes make a movie marathon out of the day while the puppies played between us. Some days, with the sun streaming in and incense in the air, it was almost nice.

But, inevitably, your daddy would have a work call, or he'd need to finish some school work, or he'd have already made plans to go see some friends, and I would be left alone again. And all of Dad's civility would disappear.

I wonder

if you died, would I feel anything?

Reading this, you might wonder why I never talked to his doctor about his behavior towards me. Especially, considering that I really thought it was a result of the illness. The thing is, I did. I talked to multiple doctors about it. Every time I reviewed the dosing - even the double-dosing or mixing medications - they said he was fine. When I mentioned his mood swings, they told me what I already knew; *of course he's lashing out. He's in pain. Just hang in there.*

And then it was August, and my IUD needed to come out.

If I'm being honest, I still wasn't ready for you. I really wasn't. I desperately wanted to be, though. Your daddy was so ready. He'd been ready for years, and I was already 34. Practically ancient in babymaking years. It seemed like now or never, and I wasn't any more ready to declare myself childfree than I was to have you.

I figured, though, it would take at least a few months to get knocked up, and by then Dad would be done with the surgery. He'd be out of pain, able to come off the pills, able to come downstairs… he'd finally be getting better. And maybe a baby was just what he needed to motivate him into restarting his life. Sure, he hadn't bonded with the new puppy, but a grandbaby? His first grandbaby? He was always droning on and on about family and legacy and what a wonderful thing it all was. So, a grandbaby? He'd get out of that damned chair of his to dance with joy!

Yes. That's it. *I'll make him a Grandpa,* I thought. *That, and the surgery, will fix everything.*

plans

the universe cradled me, kissed
me soft, and lifted my chin
with her hand.
"It's beautiful," she murmured.
"but no."

Twenty-Three

Dad's surgery was in the beginning of September. Even though we had to drive down at six thirty in the morning, I was excited to see the hints of red and orange on the leaves, and to feel the frigid air. I couldn't help but fantasize about the holidays; they'd be so much happier this year with Dad finally well and me, hopefully, pregnant.

The surgery itself took longer than expected, but everything went well. The surgeon was pleased, and the aftercare nurses all fawned over Dad. He was still a little loopy from the anesthesia, but seemed in a hopeful mood as the doctor told us that, in some rare cases, the effect might not be permanent and we'd need to retry the surgery.

"But even if that is the case," he said, "it's a minor procedure. Some patients come in once a year as needed."

On the way home, Dad struggled with nausea. It was impossible to drive any smoother in city traffic, so I opened his window for him and watched the still–crisp air brush against his face. Normally, he enjoyed the cold, but today he complained it was too much.

His voice was quiet, like a half-asleep child's, and I was completely overwhelmed with how small he suddenly seemed. When had this mountain of a man become so fragile? I pulled a blanket from the back and held him wrap up for the rest of the ride home.

The next few days were pretty great. He was able to eat without pain, consistently, for the first time in over a year. His appetite was insatiable, and I could understand it. Sure, his diet hadn't exactly been healthy all this time, but it had been restricted. He'd only eat a few certain foods, from a few certain places.

But now? Now he wanted to eat pineapple jalapeno pizza again. He wanted full dairy ice cream and extra large milkshakes, and he nearly danced at the idea of soda. I tried to remind him that he was supposed to take it easy, and that he still had a host of other digestive issues to be mindful of, but I figured a little indulgence wouldn't hurt.

By the third day, he'd stopped medicating so heavily. He didn't want to be fuzzy anymore, he said, and he started getting up and around his room. He asked me to help him dust off the curtains and rearrange his books, and he started talking about getting out of the house again. "Maybe I could talk your brother into a road trip," he pondered. He even started coming back downstairs. For a minute, there was laughter in the house again.

Your daddy, I think in retrospect, was just humoring my optimism, but we would talk about life getting back to normal. While Dad indulged in fried chicken and shakes, I indulged in imagining our new life. One where Dad was happy and laughing, where we were able to leave him for a few days to go on vacations or maybe take you camping, where we could go on date nights and leave you safely with him. It would be perfect.

A joyous world where you are surrounded by my family, and they love you because they love me. Sometimes, if I close my eyes and focus, I can still see it: my beautiful dream.

It took a couple weeks. But, eventually, Dad's indulgence caught up with him, and he refused to go back to moderation. First, his stomach went; gut rot plagued him, and he got nauseated. Then, his IBS rose up, furious at his food choices. He started medicating more heavily, and the pot threw his GERD into play.

He started taking xanax again to stave off panic attacks from the pain, then started taking sleeping pills at random intervals again. He refused to eat, or would only eat what hurt him. It all happened so quickly and, at the end of another few weeks, he was back in a place of **I don't care**.

I wanted to scream at him. I wanted to get right in his face, to shove him back in his chair and scream; *I am right here. I am right here sacrificing everything to help you and love you and you give a bigger shit about a hamburger than me? You suddenly have the will to live when you can eat spicy foods? You'll get out of bed for a chocolate shake, but not for me? Why can't you even pretend I am enough of a reason to try?*

I didn't say anything, though. I just sat in the basement and cried.

Shortly thereafter, the surgery reversed altogether. Or, at least we thought that's what had happened. The pain in his chest was back, and his heart rate was through the roof. I went through the motions and scheduled another surgery, but I didn't really see the point.

They'd warned us this could happen, and they'd warned us overeating could make it more likely. Sure, they'd take our money for another surgery, but, by now, I seriously doubted it would fix anything. I was starting to think, more and more, that Dad was destined to stay sick.

And then I was pregnant.

Two pee sticks and a blood test confirmed it.

It was just the miracle I needed. We had not been trying for more than a month, but there you were, ready to light up my life. Ready to remind Dad that life had more than pizza to offer. He might not care about me, but you? You would be his everything. I knew it.

I wanted to wait to tell everyone else, but not Dad. I needed to tell him immediately. I needed to see his eyes light up, like I knew they would, when I told him he was going to be a granddaddy. I needed to see him smile and be proud that I'd be bringing life into the house and carrying on his genes. And I *knew* he would be. It wasn't even a question.

He'd be proud of me, just as proud as that day when he showed off my calf muscles, and he'd remember that I was someone he loved.

Your daddy sat next to me, and we told him. He did smile, and he said all the right things, and he hugged each of us tight, and he teased over how fast it had happened. But I couldn't help but notice the smile never touched his eyes, and he reached for his vape pen right after we told him, and he asked us to leave after just a few minutes instead of us staying to watch TV like normal.

As we left to go back to the basement, I laughed with your daddy about Dad's response. I spun it that he seemed happily shocked, as was I, and that I couldn't wait to see him hold his grandbaby.

Quietly, though, there was a voice whispering the same thing over and over inside my head. I did my best to ignore it over the next few days as it got just a little louder: *something is wrong. We're not safe here. We have to leave.*

Twenty-Four

I did not feel safe again until a couple weeks into your fourth month. You had finally started sleeping at regular intervals, and I would get these moments of peace. For just a few seconds, the universe would offer up the briefest flash of what life could be: quiet in a way I'd never known before. With each flash, I felt myself breathe a little fuller and sink my feet into this new ground a little more.

making pancakes

I love the simplicity
of eggs, milk, and flour.
the way they dance together
in the bowl, transforming
from strangers to home.
        that's what I am, I think:
an egg
cracked wide. becoming
more.

When I found out your Daddy had to travel for work, I was almost excited at the idea. Sure, I was anxious and panicked and terrified, but also excited. I felt like I was constantly either falling apart or trying to show that everything was normal even when he was telling me I didn't have to pretend.

I found myself wondering; what would I be like with no one to pretend for? What would it be like to just be ... with you?

The fact that I had no idea was weirdly thrilling.

I expected to cry when he left for the airport, but I didn't. I expected the panic to wash over me and drown me firmly in the Bad Place. But that didn't happen, either. I felt the loss of his absence, but not in the deep and desperate way I had anticipated. Instead, I picked you up and we padded around the house as I appraised things with new eyes.

I surprised myself by, almost immediately, cleaning out the closet. As I held the pieces, trying to discern what fit or needed a rewashing, I told you about the memories behind each, and you babbled back.

we talk

all day long. a conversation
my body understands
completely
even if I don't.
still...
it's hard to deny:
to the untrained ear,
we are velociraptors

playing marco polo
(badly).

That afternoon, I decided to be extra brave
and take everyone for a walk.

miracle

What an amazing feat:
the walk. Boychild
cuddles in his carrier, his eyes wide
at the colors of fall. The dogs play
with their leashes, bite
at the wind.
Only ten minutes,
but they are glorious.

We still had frozen food our friends had
dropped off, so dinner was easy. I propped you
with a bottle and me with a dish, and we watched
some television with the dogs at our feet. It all
felt so normal. Not easy, exactly, but simple.

I reminded myself that I'd been watching
infants for nearly all my life, and the only thing
that made any of this unbearable was the stupid
ppd. My shrink and obgyn had both said, all
along and often, that it receded quicker the
quicker you started treating it. Sitting on the
couch, feeling calm and not completely
exhausted, I couldn't help but wonder: was I

finally getting better? We'd been alone all day, and I hadn't been anxious or crying in hours.

When your daddy called that night, I was beaming. "I think I can do this," I said.

"Well, I know that," he teased. He sounded tired and relieved.

"No, like, really do this. Like maybe you won't come back to a shell of a person."

I could hear the smile on his voice when he said "I love you."

I got off the phone, gave you a bath, and curled around you to settle into sleep. You fell asleep easily enough, as did I, but then you woke up. Again and again. Instead of sleeping for two or three hours, you were back to your newborn routine; you were screaming at me every forty-five minutes and taking nearly as long to fall back down.

You'd been short-circuited somehow, back to your factory settings, and nothing I could do or say could remind you that "yes, little one, you are a creature who knows how to sleep."

Somewhere around two am, I felt myself sliding back to the Bad Place, but, for the first time, your daddy wasn't there to save us. I noticed the shadows in the corners of the room growing ever so slightly larger, and it was getting harder to hear anything that wasn't you. My skin started to itch in that way that made me want to peel it off.

I closed my eyes, and tried to remember it was just the ppd. I tried to remember that I had survived three months of you; I could do one more night.

When that didn't work, I tried to think of who I could call. Only, there wasn't anyone close by who I trusted enough to see me like I was - wild hair, dead eyes, last night's tears caked on my dirty skin. I might have considered my best friend, but she was on the other side of the country. I might have considered your grandma, but she lived hours away. Nobody else could be trusted to understand; they'd judge me, or take you, or both.

Failure. Failure. Failure.

In retrospect, I should have trusted someone. We had many friends worthy of it. But I was too embarrassed, insecure, ashamed. I did survive it, though, in spite of the screaming - both from you and from the inside of my own head. Then, somehow, morning came.

this afternoon

I find myself
pouring coffee grounds directly
into brownie batter, and eating it with
a large wooden spoon. but it's
ok, because
existential dread and swaying with you while
singing
"mommy's here. she's always here"
burns calories.

That evening, when your daddy called, I tried my best to straddle the line between sugar-coating and dishonesty. I told him about showering on my own and about the pretty things we saw while walking. I told him you were struggling to sleep, but surely you wouldn't have two bad nights. And yes, I was napping when you did, and yes I was drinking something other than coffee, and yes I would call him if I wanted to hurt myself, and yes I loved him. So much.

You, though? Not so much.

It was another sleepless night, and the shadows were not growing slowly anymore. They spewed from the corners of my mind, angry and unapologetic, and crawling along the walls. I closed my eyes and tried to listen to the bees inside my skull. Did I want to hurt us yet? Was I that far gone?

No. I wasn't. My skin was itchy, and I wanted to scream, but I didn't want to hurt us. I wasn't that far into the Bad Place. Not yet. But, if I felt things for much longer, I knew I would be. So, I took a big breath and let myself numb out, dissociate, and disappear.

"It's going to be okay." I said it as much for me as for you. "We will survive this. We can do this for your daddy."

That afternoon, I had a scheduled session with my shrink. I could tell from her voice that she was concerned. She pushed me to see if there is anyone I knew who can come over, but between other people's emergencies and distances, at this point, they legitimately could not. I ran through the list of possibilities and explanations with her. Reluctantly, she agreed.

"Remember. You can set him down in a safe space and walk away. You can put the bassinet next to the bed and nap at least. You will be okay," she told me.

I told her I understood, and the logic made sense. I did not tell her, though, that the logic didn't matter; I literally could not sleep away from you. I did not tell her that I needed to feel you breathe against me. I needed to hear your breath in my ear. I needed to know you were okay. I did not tell her the real truth; I would stay awake and numb forever if it meant that you were okay. Because I was your mother. And that was what good mothers do.

That evening, your daddy promised me that you would sleep eventually. He reminded me that you were healthy and healthy babies slept. Eventually. It was just a rough few nights. "Everything will be okay," he promised. I nodded and did my best to believe him.

He was wrong.

We were a few hours into the night. I had us curled up on the couch, and in the dark living room, the blue light from the television flickered across your scream. I tried to rock you, feed you, soothe you, and then you … weren't you. It happened as fast as lightning.

I just… looked down and your eyes weren't yours. They were black. Cavernous. Your mouth stretched wider than it ever had before, twisted and screaming; I watched, horrified, as shadows poured out of it and onto my skin. They wrapped around my hands, my arms. They felt like a cold, wet wind.

"It's not you," I said. I tried to say it loudly, strong. But it was barely a whimper. "I know this is a hallucination," I whispered. "A fucking scary hallucination but that's all it is. It's. Not. Real. I can do this."

I turned the brightness up on the television and turned the bathroom light on so that it shone down the hall without completely lighting the room. I held you carefully, and avoided looking directly at you. Instead, I clocked the shadowmen who were now waiting in the corners. They stood silently, and something about their presence was comforting. After all, I'd seen them before. I knew them. They never hurt me. And even if they were just in my head, too, they made me feel less alone.

I called your daddy. The shame I felt over being so crazy tumbled out of me until I was shaking hard with waves of panic. I had to set you down beside me on the couch, careful to cradle you around with blankets so that you wouldn't fall. From the other side of the country, through the phone, your daddy spoke low and soft, like someone would to a wounded animal.

"He's okay." I said. The words came choking out. "But I'm not. I'm not okay. I'm not okay."

Failure. Failure. Failure.

"I'm so sorry," I gasped. I said it over and over between the sobs.

Failure. Failure. Failure.

He stayed on the phone with me until I could breathe and slowly bring my eyes to match yours. And there you were, my gorgeous boy, looking back sleepily at me while you worked greedily at a bottle I did not remember getting you.

I got off the phone and we settled into the couch with the dogs sentinel at my feet and the shadowmen silent along the walls.

Against all odds, eventually, we slept.

In the morning, with the sun streaming through the sliding glass doors, I was calm. However, I knew it was fleeting. I was living in the breath between unwell and lost. Something had to be done. I called your daddy as promised, and he agreed when I offered to call a postpartum doula.

Originally, it seemed like a rich lady's luxury. We weren't drink-milk-for-dinner-poor, but we weren't far from it, either. Every week, there was a new bill from the hospital, or a more expensive formula you needed, or a dog medication refill. After years of taking care of Dad instead of my own financial health, I'd just recently filed bankruptcy, and your daddy's credit cards inched closer to maxed every day.

But the truth was screaming itself at us; pay for this now or pay for hospitalization later because I was not going to survive.

So, I called. I was honest: I am alone. I am exhausted. I am hallucinating. Yes, the baby is safe.

188

They couldn't come until the following day. "Will you be alright?" she asked. Her name was Monica. I remember because I'd been watching Friends on repeat and appreciated the synchronicity. I looked down at you, still rubbing your eyes with sleep.

"Yes," I said. I was surprised at the conviction in my voice. "We can do this."

Twenty-Five

Monica came over the following day, and I could tell from the way she walked into the door, surveyed the room, and pulled you gently from my arms that she was made for this work. Even the dogs, normally protective and jumping at strangers, seemed comfortable with her. I eased myself into the nearest chair; I had forgotten what it was like to be relaxed with anyone other than your daddy.

With you on her hip, she fixed me something to eat, and she asked about our birth story. It came out in quick sentences and awkward apologies - I'd never shared the whole thing with anyone before - and I felt something lighten inside myself when I was done. As I talked, she did a few dishes and picked up some old bottles. I pushed back tears, thinking *this is what most women have. This is what a normal mom might have done.*

She suggested that I take a shower, but I could hardly stand anymore. The idea of taking off clothes, getting wet, drying off, and putting clothes back on was as ludicrous as if she'd suggested I go for a run. Or dance on the moon. Instead, I fell onto the bed and clawed my way under the covers, swaddling myself tightly in them. I listened as she popped you into a carrier and prepared to take you for a walk. "Oh it's a beautiful day," she cooed. "You and I are going to have a wonderful time." The dogs didn't even bark at her. Before the front door was shut, they were both wrapped around me.

Three hours later, I was almost a person again. Once she was sure I'd eaten something, she handed you back to me and headed home. She asked if I wanted to schedule another person to come in the morning, but I assured her that your daddy would be back by then. She left me her number just in case.

The rest of the day went by quietly.

That night, blessedly, you slept.

In the morning, I made myself coffee and waited. Your daddy came home a few hours later and hugged me tighter than I thought possible as my whimpers turned to the kind of sobbing that no amount of comfort can control. He held on as my knees buckled, and we settled onto the floor while I let out something like a scream. I tried to look up, to make sure you were safe, but he stopped me. "He's ok," he whispered. "You did it. He's safe in his bouncer and I'm home. It's all over now."

missing pieces

I bury
my head in your chest, pushing until I
feel
rib against flesh.
I want to cut

your heart
open -
feel it
swallow
me
whole.

Eventually, everything except my bladder ran dry. I picked myself up and plodded to the bathroom, watching him smile at you as I went. Sometimes, his love for you felt literally blinding. It hurt. Like I was a shadow myself, trying to survive in the middle of the sun.

I sat down and sighed.

When I got up, I noticed I was bleeding.

I felt an unusual, sharp pain in my lower stomach. Then, as I went to wipe, I felt a string. I looked down, and it reached all the way into the water. My IUD had broken loose and was now hanging out of me. I pulled it the rest of the way out and felt it tear along the sides of my vagina.

"Well at least I was able to push something out, I guess."

Twenty-Six

I was waiting for Dad to come out of his second surgery. It was early October, and I was just pregnant enough for it to be impossible to find a comfortable position in the hospital's waiting room chair. In a lot of ways, I was physically lucky; I wasn't throwing up, or dealing with insomnia, or overly fatigued. But my hips constantly felt like they were pulling apart. I felt like an old barbie doll with rotting rubber bands, and those flimsy plastic chairs were not helping matters.

Like the first one, the second surgery went well, but the doctor was very clear; they could not try again for at least six months. Dad would have to take it very easy, both with exercise and how he ate. Still woozy from the anesthesia, Dad nodded profusely. I went through the motions of being hopeful.

On the way home, I was reviewing the aftercare notes with him as he came out of his stupor, and we were talking about all the many follow up appointments that I would need to take him to. I fished for a bit of kindness; "maybe I'll get a porta potty installed in the car," I teased. "I swear this kid is already fucking with my bladder."

"Yeah," he agreed. He smiled, but his voice was humorless. "It was pretty stupid timing."

In retrospect, it was naive, but at the time, I had expected Dad to appreciate me more once I was pregnant. I guess my logic stemmed from the way he talked about Mom. He hated her, vehemently, but he always spoke fondly of her when referring to her own pregnancies. It was the only time he spoke kindly of her. He always seemed to understand how hard it was on her; he seemed to get that it was a sacrifice on her part to allow another soul to temporarily take up residence in her abdomen. I thought that if he could be compassionate for her - a woman he routinely referred to as She Who Must Not Be Named - then he would be compassionate for me.

It was getting clearer, though, that this wouldn't be the case.

I stayed silent for the rest of the drive. Once I was back home, I retreated to the safety of the basement and opened my phone. Since I didn't have a mom or grandma or sister, and none of my friends had babies, I was relying heavily on a few communities of internet strangers to feel less alone in the science experiment that is pregnancy. It was comforting to read about their morning sickness, their compulsions to buy baby clothes, and their worries over boring things like what color should they paint the crib.

I was most comfortable with Reddit, and, in a moment of kismet, that evening, the analytics recommended a new space for me: a subreddit for people with narcissistic parents. I immediately thought of mom, and I wondered if being reminded of her awfulness would make me miss her less. It did, to a degree. But, that soon became besides the point. Over the next week or so of scrolling, I found myself grappling with something else instead; according to all the resources, my father was a stone cold narcissist, and I was the family scapegoat.

I wasn't sure what I was more ashamed of: that my father was like this or that I hadn't seen it before.

I couldn't stop staring into the never-ending feed of people, just like me, squirming under terrible dictators of parents, desperate for approval and love. I read post after post, searching for some difference - some piece of proof to show to myself that *my* dad was different, that *my* dad was just having a bad day, month, year. But the more I looked, the more I felt like I was staring into a mirror.

I finally broke down and confided in your daddy. "Babe," I whispered, bereft. "I think my dad is a narcissist."

He looked at me with the sweetest, softest eyes. "Hon," he said gently, "how is this news to you?"

Over the next few weeks, it was as if someone had revealed the damned matrix to me. The more I read and learned, the more I saw his patterns, and the more I was offended by the banality of it all. I'd always thought my dad was smart. Very smart. But now I could see... he was as unoriginal as my stepfather. He was like every other narcissist out there; he couldn't even be bothered to learn new ways to hurt me. He was just pressing the same old buttons over and over again.

His favorite button was still my weight and eating habits. As soon as I got pregnant, I told him he was not allowed to comment on what I ate anymore. But that didn't stop him from noticing my body. At one point, we were all upstairs and watching television when he, rather sweetly, told me I looked "just like mom when she was pregnant." I thanked him for the compliment. Then, he added, "Of course, she was nearly nine months pregnant then."

I was only three months along at the time. "Of course," I said, almost amused at the predictability.

I started noticing other things, too. Like how he always made me sit closer to him than I was comfortable with. Or how he'd always ask for a hug, or a kiss on the forehead, but in this icky saccharine way that wasn't asking at all. Or how he'd demand I look at him when he was speaking. How long had he - this supposed pinnacle of feminism - been ignoring my bodily autonomy? Since I moved in? Since I was married? My whole life?

"I don't want to sit on the ottoman next to you," I told him one afternoon. "I am comfortable here." I offered a diffusing smile, so frustrated that something this small had me this anxious.

"Well if you're not going to watch *with* me," he pouted, "then you may as well not bother. You probably have *more interesting* things to do anyway."

I remembered what the forums had told me: do not take the bait. So, I smiled at him and nodded. "Okay then," I said. "I will bring up some food in a few hours, and you can text if you need anything."

Every time I pushed, he pushed back. But I was determined. I was going to have boundaries, he was going to respect them, and we were going to be a happy family dammit. I just needed to be strong. I could find a way to lifehack this situation even if it brought me to tears. *I can stubborn my way through anything,* I thought.

I know. It's ridiculous.

How your daddy didn't loose his mind watching me kill myself trying to do the impossible will never cease to amaze me.

I started to falter when Dad purposefully hotboxed me. He hadn't tried to do it since I announced the pregnancy, and I thought I'd finally broken him of the habit. He knew the rules; keep the windows open, or I am leaving the room. No excuses. But on this particular day, when I'd left briefly to move the laundry, he had not just closed the curtains; he'd closed the window, too.

I didn't realize until my vision blurred.

"It's fine," he told me when I realized, "parents got stoned all the time not that long ago. It," he said, pointing at my belly, "is fine. You needed to relax anyway." He chuckled.

It shocked me straight into dissociation. As I watched myself leave the room, eyes dry and face blank, I heard a voice from somewhere: *should we just leave?*

We went back and forth like this for all of November.

Then, he had a heart attack.

Oddly, what I remember most isn't the screaming that came after - the night I've already told you about. What I remember most is the calm and relief I felt leaving him behind at the hospital the night before. I remember how that feeling stuck to me, like the softest of blankets, that entire night that he was gone.

It was the first night in at least four years where I wasn't worried: that he'd need something, ask for something impossible, demand something unpleasant or unsafe or illegal, wake me or yell at me or both. I wasn't worried. About anything. At all.

The feeling was so unfamiliar I had a panic attack anyway.

Twenty-Seven

It took hours after your daddy came home
from his trip that day for me to completely
believe he was there. I kept turning around
corners, expecting you and I to be alone again. I
would hold my breath as I walked into the
bedroom, expecting to see his side of the closet
still empty. Every time I went to touch him, a part
of me worried I was hallucinating again and that
my fingers would slip straight through.

I don't remember asking

but your daddy says
it's ok -
they'll let him
work from home.
he sounds resolved. calm. but,
I see fear.

I had fallen into the same dark water as when
you were born: the Bad Place. But, it was a little
faster swimming back to where I could stand this
time. After a few days, I started to catch my
breath again. Then, as if the universe was

rewarding my determination, your daddy told me he'd gotten some news; he'd landed a new job that wouldn't make him travel at all. He was just waiting for them to find a contract, and then he'd start. "Last time was the last time," he told me. "You won't ever have to do that again."

While I swam back to the proverbial shore, I thought about my mother. Alot. I remembered Dad mentioning, many years ago, that she had ppd when I was born. He'd say how she could never stand the sound of my crying, or how she could never get me to sleep; she'd always be so pissed when he would pick me up and I'd settle right down. When I was younger, I'd always thought those stories were proof that he loved me more from the very start, somehow. Now, they resonated differently.

now I know

why my mother can't
love me:
she was drowning. (like me)
she needed
love
to light her
way to the surface. she needed
mouths, outstretched and tender, to lend her
air along the way. but, she
was all
alone.

I wondered again... did she hate me so much for leaving her not because I'd left, but because I'd left *for him?* I thought about you - this partial person I only sort of liked; if you suddenly took up a relationship with my father and told me you needed space from me, would I be able to stand it? Would I be able to be a good enough mom to give you the space to pick someone who'd hurt me so terribly? And what would that feel like if I actually loved you through and through, the way a mother should? Would I end up hating you, too?

I wanted to say no. But honestly... I didn't know.

I couldn't stop thinking about it. I kept mulling our relationship over and over in my mind, looking for some sort of clue that *this* was the root of the problem.

Sure, she'd been awful at my brother's wedding. And, there was a history of shitty behavior on her part. But, to be fair, I've been a bitch to her over the years, too. I mean, no one can hurt their mother like a daughter can, right? Once, I told her I would stop mothering my brothers when she finally bothered to do it her damn self. Another time, I uninvited her to my wedding after she paid for the dress (which I returned but she still had to eat the cost on). I have called her names and pushed her buttons and taken satisfaction in her rage just as she has mine.

But, as I mentioned earlier, I've also tried the opposite. I've groveled over Thanksgiving dinners, apologized at Passovers, and I've made god only knows how many compromises over terse cups of coffee in neutral locations. I've made gifts and concessions, and I am always civil when we wind up in the same room together.

Neither approach ever ends up in anything other than heartache. For both of us. I knew this. I know this. And yet.

I kept thinking about how much time had passed, and how she loves babies, and how we'd finally have something to bond over. I didn't expect a doting grandmother out of her, exactly, but maybe she'd be willing to hug you long enough for me to pee? Maybe she'd tell me how long it took to recover from tearing and commiserate with me about how insensitive the majority of gynecologists are? Maybe we'd laugh about that one time she took six year old me with her to her pap smear and she yelped so loud at the cold speculum that I yelled at the doctor and then she started giggling so hard the doctor had to remove it and start all over.

Maybe she'd finally understand that I *didn't* understand: I didn't know who Dad really was, and if I had, I would have played things differently, and please… please could she take pity on me just long enough to let the past die?

I wrote dozens of letters. But every time I started to send one, I couldn't get over the last time I'd seen her face: that day at the wedding. She'd tried to stay focused on the festivities, on my brother, her new daughter in law, anything and everything but me. But, occasionally, I'd notice her eyes drift towards me and all I saw was fear. Yes, she was horrible to me, but she looked truly terrified. Of me. Of everything.

At the time, I hadn't understood it. But, I did now. I recognized her fear; she was stuck in the Bad Place, and she'd been there so long, nothing I could do would ever pull her out. So, I never sent the letters. I decided to do what seemed like the kindest thing, what my brother had asked me to do when I'd told him I was pregnant in the first place, "she's been through enough," he'd begged, "Just leave her alone."

I tell my shrink

it's like I'm
walking
on broken glass
towards a light
I cannot see
but
everyone
promises is there.

Even though I remained skeptical that I'd ever truly be free of my depression again, I marveled at the fact that, unlike my mother, I'd found a way out of the deepest end twice now. It only seemed logical, then, that if I ended up back there, I could

find my way home a third time. I could swim
back as many times as it took to get back to you.
Your daddy would help me. My shrink would
help me. I knew it in my bones. I wouldn't end up
like Mom. I wouldn't end up like those lost
parents who never have the chance to treat their
ppd or ppa, who live their entire mothering lives
living in shadows.

It would hurt like hell, but I could survive. We
would find our way. Again and again if we had to.

a new noise

you are staring out the window, eyes tight on a
squirrel. Your mouth opens, struggling and
empty.

and then

the most delicious laughter.

Twenty-Eight

One of the few advantages of my ppd was that I didn't really care about developmental milestones. Don't misunderstand; I wanted you to be healthy, of course. I just wasn't overly invested in the specifics. Friends teased that I acted more like a second time mom than a first timer. But, there was a sort of truth to it.

After all, I'd spent the majority of my teens taking care of infants, and I knew enough to know that you all sort of develop when you damn well please. There's not a lot of rhyme or reason to when a particular potato decides to roll over, or sit up, or decide it's fun to practice screams. Instead of feeling like a failure every time you declined to hit a developmental milestone right on target, I felt more like an anthropologist studying an alien species.

"Today," I'd say aloud to absolutely no one, "he seems to be considering whether or not tummy time is worth the effort. To his left, there's a small orange spoon. To his right, a ball of lint. Hmm... the ball of lint seems to be winning his attention, but will he wriggle towards it? No. not today. Today, it is easier to scream until his dim-witted caregiver retrieves it. Understandable."

I found meal times particularly entertaining.

Given the fact that you were enormous (99th percentile in both height and weight), our pediatrician let us start you on solid foods at four months. At first, you'd stare down the spoon with the sort of skeptical glare I'd expect from a hardened news anchor, but now, at five months old, you were insatiable. The bigger the flavor, the better: avocados with Old Bay, broccoli with enough garlic to make my eyes water, eggs with hot sauce, miso paste straight from the bin and pickled anything always.

I love to cook, and it was so satisfying to see someone excitedly devour what I had made. I'd buy those little cans of baby food, give them a good zhuzhing, and see what you wanted to try. It would be quite some time before you'd be eating enough solids to even consider giving up the bottle, but I was delighted by how fearless you were. I'd heard horror stories of kids living on four or five foods, refusing anything else, and here you were - ready to try anything.

Unfortunately, that attitude came with a price: heartburn.

After a weekend of endless screaming and wet burps, I took you to the pediatrician. When I told her what you'd been eating, she giggled at me. Giggled. "That's some appetite, little boy. You'll outgrow us all." I remember her poking at your little belly and feeling overwhelmed with the urge to snap her thin finger. Was she seriously teasing you about your weight while you were in pain?

Thankfully, I kept myself in check long enough to get your prescription. We also bought some probiotics and gas drops - all the gas drops. And we stopped with the hot sauce. Temporarily, anyway.

I found it interesting: it was so easy for me to adjust routines for your health and wellness. I hadn't given it a second thought. Sure, you're thinking, that's what a mom is supposed to do. But remember - most days, I still wasn't feeling much like a mom at all. Maybe for a few hours here or there you felt like mine, but still - even at five months old - you were some strange kid I was being forced to watch without pay or bathroom breaks. You were, mostly, an adorable inconvenience.

And yet.

Without even really thinking about it, I switched up your foods, your sleeping arrangements (I propped us up), your bottle preparation, and the way you sat in your bassinet all for the sake of this new health issue.

Why the fuck couldn't I do the same for myself?

Why couldn't I be as kind to myself as I could to you? The monster who ruined my body in the first place.

I was sitting on the couch, and I remember taking the moment to feel my body - really feel her. You know what? She fucking hurt. Everywhere. My right hip was out of alignment again. My left knee kept trying to pop out. My lower back was swollen with pain, and my stomach felt distended and cold. How had I not noticed that my head ached until just now? And when had my neck gotten so tight I couldn't look fully left?

What. The. Fuck.

I thought I was going to start taking care of myself. Hadn't I just declared that to the world? Hadn't I started doing stretches and squats here and there? Why wasn't I committing? Why wasn't I following through?

I got up and walked over to your daddy. "I gained a hundred pounds for this little fucker and I'm sick of needing to groan to get off the couch. I am going to find a way to start liking myself again. I mean it this time."

"Why are you saying this like I'm going to argue with you?" he asked.

"Because it feels stupid," I admitted, suddenly feeling very vulnerable. "It feels stupid to say that I don't like myself. That I ... I can't be bothered to be as loving to myself as I am to this little terrorist. That I don't love myself as much as I love him when I barely love him at all...." I was whispering now, irritated at how intimate the conversation had turned.

"Well, it's not stupid to want to take care of yourself," he offered, his voice kind. "The rest of what you just said is, honestly, pretty dumb. But sometimes we have to say really dumb things to get to the smart stuff. And you are one of the smartest people I know."

I puffed up a little at the compliment and padded back to the couch, notepad in hand, determined to find a way to be the kind of person I wanted to be.

And then a weird thing happened.

My mother's house burned down.

Seriously. The following day, I happened to call a good friend of mine. She lives one street down from my mother, in the same house she lived in as a child. "There's smoke," she said, as she stepped out of her house to get the mail. "A lot of it."

While still on the phone, she padded down the street, trying to see where it was coming from. "It's got to be a house fire," she mused, "oh I hope everyone is okay. It's on your old street," she exclaimed. "I'm going to go up and see who it is." I listened as she climbed the hill at the bottom where her street met mine and mused about whose house it might be, running down the list of everyone who lived on the street those days. Then, her breath caught short.

"Oh my god. Sweetie. It's your mom."

The fire engines were roaring up to the scene just as she got there. I could hear them in the background. "Oh jeeze," she whispered. "It's completely ruined."

"Is everyone okay?" I asked.

"Here. Someones here," she said. She called over to another neighbor. They lived across the way. I overheard in pieces as they explained they'd seen the fire and called the fire department.

"She's at work," my friend said. "Your mom's not here."

"Are the dogs okay," I asked. Mom had two that I knew of. She adored them as much as I did mine.

"Yeah," she said. "They were in the backyard." I listened to her sigh. "It looks like they're close to putting it out now, but, God. The whole back of the house is gone. It's just gone."

"You should go," I said. We said our goodbyes and then I got off the phone. I stood there, still, thinking of the loss.

People always say "it's just stuff," but it's not. Not really. It's the way your grandmother's afghan is just the right kind of scratchy and makes you feel safe when it's wrapped around you. It's the way the old photo album smells like your dad's cologne and every time you get a whiff, you're right back with him at the park feeding ducks and laughing about the day. It's the Christmas ornament you bought when you were pregnant, still full of all the hope and optimism you had for your unborn babe. Some things transcend their forms and become... love.

Now, my mom had lost it all, and I ached for her.

I remembered a few pictures I had tucked away; a picture of her grandmother and grandfather, as well as one of her great aunt. I also had a few of her, and her mother, and her sister. Maybe a dozen all together. It wasn't much, but it was more than she now had. So, later that week, your daddy scanned them in and we emailed from his account over to an old address of hers that I had.

I thought for days about what I should say.

Dear Mom,
I'm so sorry. I'm sorry for your loss, and I'm sorry that hearing from me is probably painful. I don't want to add to the heartache I know you're feeling. Truly. But if I were you, I'd want to have these... so, I've attached a copy of the few photos of you and the family that I have. I hope they bring at least a little comfort.
Love, Me

I figured there was a chance I'd hear from her, but not a very good one. After all, her house just burned down. I seriously doubted she had the time or emotional energy to deal with me, and that was okay. Honestly, it was kind of preferable. I waited a few days, anxiously, to see if we'd hear anything, but nothing came. It occurred to me she might be so busy she wouldn't even be checking her personal email. Maybe she didn't even use that account anymore. After another day or so, I decided it was for the best and stopped thinking about it.

The following day, your daddy came in with a dark look on his face. "You should probably read this," he said, offering his phone to me, "but I don't really want you to since it's just going to upset you."

As I reached for the phone, I figured it was something from Mom. It wasn't. Instead, it was my aunt. For a bit of reference, when I left back in my teens, I had sort of assumed my aunt would have had my back. I'd always had a connection with her; we talked on the phone regularly, we traded letters back and forth - she just seemed to get me. Unfortunately, I'd misread the situation; she was, in actuality, one of the most vicious when I left. Additionally, over the years, as my relationship with Mom came and went, her criticism stayed constant.

So, I wasn't surprised at what she'd written even as it hurt. The general gist of the email was "how dare I and fuck off and never reach out to us again." It went on for two pages. I think what surprised me the most was that she found the time to write two pages of vitriol. I mean, her sister's house had just burned down. Didn't she have things to do?

Then, quietly, underneath the surprise, guilt started to fester and I started beating myself, proverbially, with the shame stick. Had I done the wrong thing? Should I have just left it alone? Did I make it worse somehow?

Sometimes, I think the hardest part of dealing with mentally ill people is never knowing if you are about to make it worse somehow. You never know if something well-meant or innocuous is going to send everything sideways. Under different circumstances, it would seem ridiculous to second guess this sort of kind gesture. All my friends agreed it had been a sweet thing to do.

But, it plagued me for days: should I have somehow known this would go wrong? Did it really hurt Mom as much as my aunt insinuated? If so, how did I not know that by now? How could I get something so kindly-meant so wrong?

Finally, I forced myself to stop thinking about it. I was never going to figure out how to take care of myself if I was obsessing over her, and no matter how much I obsessed I was never going to figure her out. So, every time I thought about her, I'd say, out loud, "knock it off. Move on," and start actively thinking about anything else.

Then, a week later, I heard from Mom herself.

She reached out to your daddy via social media, asking after you. Could she see a picture, she wanted to know. Would we consider having you in her life, she was curious. Mostly, she said, "I just want to know he's okay."

I wrote back immediately: "you and your sister need to get on the same page. Less than two weeks ago she told me to never speak to you again. Now you want to talk. Make up your mind."

She promised that I would not hear from my aunt again. When we asked if Josh was still talking to Dad, she confirmed that he was. I wasn't surprised; Josh had maintained a relationship with *her* after I'd stopped, why wouldn't he do the same with Dad? I wrote that, under no circumstances, could she share pictures with Josh.

I was terrified Josh would show them to Dad, who would then try to find us. Every time the maintenance man, or apartment manager, knocked on the door, I would panic at the idea that Dad had finally found us and would try to sue for grandparents' rights to see you just to spite me.

I read it twice before I sent it, making sure I was clear: "If you share any of this with Josh, we will stop this immediately. You will never hear from us, or about him, again."

Mom responded almost immediately; she was emphatic. "I understand. It's been too long," she wrote. "I am not about to let your father, or your brother's support for him, get in the way of knowing you or my grandchild."

I tried to stay guarded. I really did. But it was impossible to put out the spark of hope starting to glow inside of me. Did she really - finally - want me? I imagined the coming spring; we could meet at a park and laugh about the horrors of birth while you played in the dirt. Or, maybe she'd meet us for coffee, and we could grimly joke about both leaving my father, like two divorcees.

I talked to your daddy about it, and he reminded me that we were still quite a long way off from all that. I agreed, of course. But what would it hurt to imagine? I hadn't dared to hope for anything more than to be left alone from this woman for years. Now, it seemed like maybe... just maybe ... I could ask for more.

I was determined to savor it.

I'm glad I did, too. Because the day after we sent over a handful of pictures, she sent this: "I have decided I am uncomfortable lying to your brother. I'm not keeping these from him. I won't stop supporting him."

It took a good two minutes for me to process what she had written. Frankly, I still can't entirely process it: I still don't understand why she thought she needed to lie to my brother. It seemed easy to me for her to simply tell him the following: *I can't show you these because she asked me not to. If you want to know your nephew, take it up with her.* Where's the lie there?

It was more than that, though.

My mother is a lot of things. But, she's not stupid. She's absentminded sometimes, and she's a klutz all the time, but she's not an idiot. So, she *knew* why I was afraid of Dad seeing pictures of you. She *knew* that he was just insane enough to try to find you based on those pictures, to show up at our door unexpectedly. She *knew* that I had once adored my father, and that if I was now afraid of seeing him and afraid of him knowing my child, then he had done something really, really wrong. She *knew* I was trying to protect you.

And she didn't fucking care. Her codependent relationship with my brother was more important to her than your safety.

It was the first time I felt, truly, like I would have set the world on fire to protect you. I would have crawled into that computer, popped out of her screen, and ripped the hair right off her head to make my point. I'd never understood what people mean when they say Mama Bear or talk about that protective mother instinct. But in that moment, it filled every part of me. I had never felt such rage.

I stayed quiet for what must have felt like forever to your daddy. I had to. The screaming in my head was too loud. After a long few minutes, it finally quieted down enough for another thought to squeeze in; *you can protect him without all that. You don't ever have to talk to her again.*

I looked down at you, bouncing on my lap, and you looked up at me. I felt surrounded by a near blissful calm. "Sorry, button," I murmured, "looks like you don't get two grandmas after all."

I turned to your daddy. "Tell her this," I said. "Tell her: 'thank you for your honesty. You will not hear from us again.' Then go ahead and block her. We're done."

Twenty-Nine

I thought I'd be sad about Mom, but I felt empowered. Powerful. With two simple sentences, I cut my mother from your life. Sure, you might choose to seek her out one day; that's your right. But, until then, you will never fear her, never miss her. You will not spend a single moment agonizing over what she wants you to do or say.

I did that.

Me.

I started to wonder - what else could I do?

falling

so slowly
I am learning the curves
of your fingers and
falling in
love with the slope
of each toe.
you are changing every minute, but
I recognize you more
and more.

I picked you up and squatted down to grab a leftover bottle. You giggled at the up and down motion. "Oh really," I teased, "you like pretending to be a medicine ball?" I lifted you high into the air, amazed my upper back and neck muscles remembered how to be both tense and open. I brought you to my chest, gave you a kiss on the head, and, being sure to keep you close in case I fell over, sat down into a deep and glorious lunge. My entire skeletal system was uncertain about the act, but it held firm. Slowly, I raised back up, and you laughed the entire time.

I managed nine more before I had to sit down. "Okay then," I panted. "It's a start."

I decided I could commit to doing that every day: 10 squats. I could even do it holding you. After a few days, I wondered; what else could I do with you? Turns out, you thought lunges were just as funny as squats. Your daddy would be on a work call at the livingroom table, and I'd quietly count us back and forth across the apartment. It was 15 lunges exactly one way.

First, we just went down. Then, down and back. After two weeks, I could do three times down and back without feeling like I was going to die, and I'd started doing the few pilates moves I remembered while holding you like a medicine ball.

It felt good.

Well, no. It felt awful.

Truly awful.

I had never been this out of shape before. Everything hurt. Absolutely everything. But it was a familiar kind of hurt. The kind of hurt I'd get after a hard session of deadlifts at the gym, or after a two hour run. The kind where your whole body is simultaneously screaming "fuck you" and "good job." And even with my muscles screaming at me, I didn't want to stop.

I refused.

Soon after, I started doing yoga again because I had to. I'd only lasted a week or so the first time. Honestly, I've never really been a big fan of yoga. But, weirdly, it's a fan of me; I've had back issues since I was a kid, and whenever it flares up, or whenever I manage to break my body in some sort of stupid way, yoga is the only thing that consistently gets me back to a pain-free existence. That and a shit-ton of ibuprofen. The only issue was I couldn't figure out how to hold you while I did it. I tried, once, and nearly catapulted you across the room during a sun salutation.

I decided to see if you'd let me set you down again like I had done before. I put you in your bouncer on the floor right at the head of my mat. Then, I leaned back into what I'm sure looked nothing like a downward dog pose. The muscle fibers running along the backs of my legs and my lower back could not quite decide whether to scream or applaud. I couldn't see you, but I heard you starting to fuss and pulled quickly out and down to a plank, my face level with yours. My arms were furious about the whole thing, but you were thrilled.

"Peekaboo," I teased. I lay my body on the floor, then I came up, ever so slowly, into a cobra until we were face to face again. "Peekaboo," I said, smiling. You erupted into giggles. They were infectious, and soon I was laughing so hard I fell over.

The stronger my body got, the more comfortable I was listening to it. I still had a terrible time doing anything, or asking anything, that was just for me. But this - getting stronger, losing weight, getting healthy - this was for you. I wanted to like myself, to love myself, so I could be a better mom for you. I wanted to be the mom who could play on the floor with you, who could run around the block with you, who could lift you up to see the lions at the zoo. You deserved it even if I didn't think that I did. So, I was forcing myself to take time, and energy, just for me. For you.

By the time Thanksgiving rolled around, your daddy's mommy - your grandma - had practically skywritten how much she wanted to see you. I wanted that for her, and for you, but the idea of a day of polite smiles and uncomfortable questions would be too much; I didn't want to keep track of who already knew about Mom or who would be uncomfortable if I was honest about Dad or who believed ppd was something I could just pray away. The sheer thought of it made my hands shake. So, your daddy took you instead.

alone time

your daddy
takes you -

shows you off
to family and friends,
where you eat your weight
in mashed potatoes and
are gone
nearly long enough
for me to miss you.

The day after, I brought out our Christmas things. It hurt. I knew it would, but I was still somehow surprised at the way my heart deflated as I held the few ornaments and cards we'd managed to bring with us. Each one carried a decades' worth of memories, and the whole box smelled of sadness.

They were still beautiful, though.

I have always loved Christmas. And Chanukah. And Yule. Any holiday where people use twinkling lights and chocolate to try to beat back the terrors of the dark seems so... human. I am a sucker for all of it.

Unfortunately, my family - specifically Dad and Josh - hated the holidays. They allowed me to decorate, to bake, and to generally make merry, but everything they "noticed" about my festivities was wrong somehow. The tree was too big or too small, the decorations were too kitsch or in the way, the cookies were too crunchy or sweet or not sweet enough. And, irritatingly, my father had a habit of eating the entire lot - saving none for me or your daddy - while complaining the entire time.

But this year would be different. This year, I'd be free to make merry in peace. From your bouncer, you watched me hang lights and smiled at the way they threw shadows around the room. I hung ornaments from the lights themselves (we couldn't afford a tree, and a tree with an infant seemed asinine anyway), and they swayed in the warm breeze flowing from the HVAC vents.

The only thing that was missing was Grandma.

visitation

all day,
the microwave
has been starting
on its own.
it's probably an electrical short -
but I am lost and
need to believe
in magic.
"hi grandma," I whisper each time and smile.
"I miss you too."

It would be the third Christmas I didn't buy her a gift, but there was still a strangeness in it. I loved watching Grandma open a comforter, or a puzzle, or a set of colored pencils only to have her eyes light up with that "how did you know," expression. As I decorated the apartment, I found myself preemptively grieving for it. But, I realized, it would also be the first Christmas that

I didn't buy either Dad or Josh a gift either, and
that brought me nothing but relief.

Oftentimes, I'd spend all year hunting for the
perfect gift, especially for Dad. I'd wander
bookstores and thrift shops, or learn how to
make things. Even when he started phoning in
his gifts to me, I kept at it. Every year, I would
find something amazing: a signed book from his
favorite author, a small statue of his favorite dog,
a piece of memorabilia that reminded him of a
special childhood place or outing, and sometimes
I'd spend real money on an expensive appliance
he'd been eyeing. I killed it. Every year. And every
year, I was met with a polite smile and lukewarm
response.

It took him years to grind me down, but
eventually, he took all the fun out of gift giving. I
realized it didn't matter - he'd never be happy.
And why do we buy gifts if not to make the
people we love happy?

But you - you were just a baby! I could toss a
pile of wrapping paper at you, and you would
legitimately be delighted. I considered it -
watching you play with whatever we gave you on
Christmas morning - and it brought on a whole
body smile. I realized I didn't want to give you
just wrapping paper. Or, if I did, it would be full of
designs you really enjoyed: planets and stars, or
dogs. And then a funny thing occurred to me: you
already had likes and dislikes. You, in all your
squishy infant glory, were already sort of a
person.

That had, honestly, never crossed my mind.

At that moment, I felt a small shifting somewhere in my body. You weren't just an obligation - a screaming, leaking bag of flour I had to constantly feed - you were a person. A tiny person, sure, with limited vocabulary and singular interests, but a person. And if you were a person, then I could get to know you. We could get to know each other. We could have fun together.

I stared at you in your bouncer. "What fun holiday thing could we do together," I asked aloud. I looked around the room, waiting until inspiration struck. My eyes settled on a stack of white cardstock peeking out from my all-but-forgotten craft cart. "We are going to make Christmas cards," I announced.

A part of me knew it was a ridiculous proposition, but I didn't care. I gathered all the materials into a basket on the table. Then, I sat down at the table and squished you into a stable position on top of my lap. I plugged in the crayon melter and waited for it to get warm. Then, I wrapped your chubby hand around mine and, together, we melted a jungle green crayola crayon into a crooked little Christmas tree.

You lasted about fifteen minutes before loudly insisting you had other places to be. At which point, I popped you down onto the floor with a few toys and finished the last couple cards. I appraised our work while you worked on pulling yourself towards one of the dogs. The cards certainly weren't amazing, but we had made them. And it had been fun.

I decided to steer into the feeling. While your daddy was out at a meeting, we strung up some more lights. Really, you just got in the way, but I genuinely enjoyed watching your eyes go wide at the way the old school bulbs glittered against the afternoon sun. Then, when I finally plugged them in, you gasped and your hands reached out; you let out a proper giggle and started belly laughing when I got them swaying back and forth. Then, we were both laughing.

my love,

Today, you came home and found
me in the rocking chair,
our son, asleep and curved against me
like a dog with his favorite
chewed-up toy.

Christmas Day that year was muted, but sweet. You had just started sitting up, and we have this hilarious picture of you sitting on the ottoman playing with some ribbon while a monster kills someone on the television in the background. I took it with the new polaroid camera your daddy gave me for the holiday, and I think it summed up my headspace nicely: I was starting to make space for the adorable, but monsters still lurked in most corners. Still, I remember sitting on the couch with your daddy, my head nestled against his neck, and thinking that this new normal didn't entirely suck. I was exhausted, but in a good way.

And you... I looked down at you and smiled, thinking *you are exhausting. But in a good way.*

new year / new you

you have resolved
to pick up phones, grab hair, outgrow clothes, call strangers, piss on everything, terrorize the plants, and laugh.

You are resolved to
more laughter
than your pillsbury body can handle,
and I -
I am resolved to you.

Thirty

When I realized I was pregnant, back before everything with Dad went truly to shit, I was immediately excited for the holidays. I had visions of a fat and happy me waddling around, decorating and making cookies, like a young Ms. Claus. As we got closer, I started hunting around for family traditions I might want to repurpose as our own, delighted with each daydream.

Would we be the kind of family that had a popsicle advent calendar? Would we make reindeer cookies? Would we be a Santa family? Each idea sent me into a delicious daydream, and it was almost enough to help me ignore the fact that Grandma was gone.

It was almost enough to make a happy holiday season.

Almost.

The moment I brought the decoration boxes out, Dad was on my case. "What the hell is even the point? It's not like it's actually here yet," he said, gesturing towards my stomach. "You are already telling me you're so tired. You never have enough time as it is."

He was right. I *was* always telling him I was so tired. But it wasn't because I actually was. It was because, other than your daddy needing me, it was the only excuse he would accept for my not spending every waking moment with him without a five minute diatribe on my general uselessness. Even my job was suspect; I'd leave him breakfast in the morning only to be met with, "aren't you going to quit when it's born anyway? Why don't you just quit now? Just call out and be done with it. We can afford it."

Setting aside the fact that I liked my job and getting out of the house, the truth was that we couldn't actually afford it. Marijuana might have been legal, but it wasn't any less expensive; Dad was spending nearly a thousand dollars every month on his pain management. Additionally, he was slipping into the habit of waking up while still on sleeping pills and going on an online shopping spree. But, instead of asking me to help prevent it from happening, he would open items he'd forgotten about with delight and eager surprise. Whenever I mentioned the budget, or told him we needed to curb his spending, he'd guilt trip me into dissociating.

It would have been bad enough if his decisions were impacting only his own bank account and credit score, but I was saddled with debt right alongside him. Back when he'd first stopped paying his bills, he went ahead and added me to his bank account. He also added me to all of his credit cards. At the time, I was too naive to understand what that meant; I thought it meant that I was authorized to act on his behalf, but anyone who understands anything about finances would know just how wrong I was. Every credit card he authorized me on was now my responsibility in the eyes of those banks. By the time I was pregnant, the majority of them were maxxed out or overdrawn.

When I realized this, and brought the debt up with Dad, his response was, "Oh what do I care if I have debt? When I die, it just goes away anyway. It's not like I'm buying a new house, or a car ever again. What's the big deal?"

"Well," I offered quietly, "I really wanted to be debt free before the baby came. I've been working really hard on my own cards. I just... even if you do die, you know I'll be responsible for your debt, right? Did you know that's how this was set up?"

"I mean," he waved a hand, "I'm responsible for your student loans. For this house. It's not like I complain about that."

"Sure," I said, "because I have life insurance for that. You know that. You wouldn't actually have to pay for any of it." I forced myself to reask the question; " But I'd have to repay for you. Did you know I'd be responsible for your cards?"

"Of course. That's how it works," he said, dismissive. "If you're so worried about it, just declare bankruptcy. It's not like they're not going to let you."

I'd considered bankruptcy in the past - shortly after a failed business venture of your daddy's - but Dad had been adamant that we take the time to dig our way out. He'd had to declare when I was a child, and he knew how impactful it could be. It wasn't something he ever expressed shame over; in fact, he was proud of the pragmatism at declaring. Still, he'd always insisted it was a

nuclear option and not to be undertaken lightly. I
wasn't sure what had changed since then.

"You know, you'll have to file as well," I said.

"Fine. I'll sign whatever you need me to. It's
not like it's that big of a deal." Then he turned his
direction back to the television and turned up
the volume.

Confession: up until this very moment, writing
this all down, I did not think filing bankruptcy
was that big of a deal. After all, from a logistical
perspective, it really wasn't. Sure, I worried that
the court would say I wasn't allowed to, and I
worried that Dad would suddenly change his
mind, and I worried that I would somehow forget
a form or fill something out incorrectly and have
to pay more money for the bankruptcy to be
granted. But, truly, the whole thing was pretty
straightforward. And, ever since Dad had filed
back when I was a kid (and then my husband
early into our marriage after the business), I
refused to cow-tow to the stigma: shit happens,
all the time, to people who are trying their best.
Screw anyone who says otherwise.

Still, while I insisted on being militantly open
with people about what I was doing, determined
to do my part to combat the social stigma, I never
exactly told people the truth, either. I couldn't
bear the shame - not that I was having to declare
bankruptcy - but that I was having to do it
because of Dad. So, instead of discussing his
financial irresponsibility, I'd say "I had to take
time off to be a caregiver, and then Dad got sick

and there were all the bills." It wasn't a lie, exactly. But it implied that the bills were medical. After all, medical costs in the US are a nightmare, everyone knows this, so no one ever asked any follow up. Instead, they'd ask how I was doing and offer sympathy.

I could not even bear to tell my lawyer the truth.

I just felt so fucking stupid.

I imagine spouses of gamblers, or addicts, feel the same way. How could I explain why I had been so willing to hand my financial health over to this man? How could I explain how he had used my trust to his advantage? How could I explain how, after all of that, I still had anything to do with him? That, in fact, I was still taking care of him and taking crap from him and wasn't sure I could even survive if I stopped. I could not bear to see the look of disgust on her face. I was disgusted enough. I was disgusting, and I was desperately trying to make sure no one else saw.

untitled #2

I am not sure
how you would react if
I suddenly
wasn't.

Christmas Day hurt that year. I was as fat as Ms. Claus, but that's as close as I got to my fantasies. Dad did not even bother to take his gifts out of their boxes. Nor did he get me anything. My brother announced he had decided to renounce Christmas as a materialistic ploy, but I couldn't help but clock his new designer clothes, the fact that he took his gifts eagerly, or that he brought Dad a new novelty marijuana pipe.

Your daddy and I tried to celebrate amongst ourselves with our favorite movies and food, but Dad pouted that we wouldn't watch something else with him and complained how we were shoving food he wasn't supposed to eat in his face. When we finally went up to bed, after Dad had been upstairs a few hours, the haze of marijuana smoke was visible. I slept on the couch in the basement.

On January 1st, I did as I do every year and took down the decorations. Usually, it's a bittersweet process; I'm always sad to see the glitter and tinsel go, sad to box up the moments of joy I've collected from thrift shops and holiday stores over the years. This year, though, I was relieved. Each bauble was a reminder that I'd been wrong; my pregnancy hadn't changed anything. If anything, it had just made things worse. I didn't understand what I had done wrong.

I held my stomach as your daddy hoisted the last of the boxes up into the attic, trying to shield you from a sadness I feared would take over my entire body and then infect yours.

A few weeks later, I went to bankruptcy court. It had taken some doing, but I'd managed to get the court to grant Dad a medical exception to appearing. I had a temporary authorization to answer questions on his behalf, and I remember that I was terrified to do, or say, something wrong. Between my panic and my pregnancy, I was on edge for the entire time it took for your daddy to drive us into the city.

The security guards were kind, and, after we got a bit turned around in the building, we found our lawyer and our seats. My lawyer was an older woman with a thick briefcase and a no nonsense attitude; she had a gorgeous black coat and amusingly unpractical heels. I remember because there was ice on the ground, and I was amazed she hadn't twisted an ankle yet. She had one of those matter-of-fact faces, like she only smiled on important occasions. When we found her, she started talking quickly, going through what would happen next and reminding me of what I needed to say.

Something about me must have caught her eye, though, because she reached out and put her hand on my elbow. She waited patiently for me to bring my eyes to hers. The kindness in them nearly brought me to tears. "You are going to be fine," she said, soft. "You have filled out all your paperwork correctly, you've answered every question I've given you, and all we are doing now is giving that same information to the court in person and those same answers to a judge. I am right here if you don't understand a question, okay? It's going to be fine."

I nodded and tried to smile. Then, she was kind enough to distract me with questions about you until it was our turn.

The judge was a soft-spoken man who smiled at my big belly. When I sat down in the chair, his smile vanished, but he was patient as I worked to stay calm. A few times, I found myself rambling, apologized, and refocused on the question. He asked why Dad wasn't there, and I struggled. It was true when I said Dad was very frail, and it would have been hard on his health to come in. It was also true when I told him there was a doctor's note on file. But as I recited all of that, it still felt like lying. It wasn't the whole truth; he didn't *want* to come, and I didn't have the chutzpah to try to force him - I'd rather have the judge call me a liar and go to jail.

He didn't, though. I would have to wait for the formal paperwork, but he tentatively agreed to grant my bankruptcy without a problem. "This is pretty straightforward," he noted. "And I'm sure you'd like to have this settled before your little one is born." His smile came back, briefly. "It's an incredible thing. I have two." Then, he was all business again. "I will need to speak to your father, though. I have a few questions."

I turned to my lawyer, panicked. She placed a hand on mine and reiterated his medical condition. After a few minutes, they agreed on a time for a phone call and that I would be allowed to participate in the call and answer questions as necessary. I knew Dad would be unhappy, but there was nothing I could do.

Four days later, I sat in Dad's room and listened as he spoke to the judge. An hour before the call, he had been an anxious wreck; "I still don't see why they need to talk to me," he lamented. "I don't know anything about this. You do all my bills, and you don't talk to me about any of it, and you just blow me off when I do ask you, so I can't even take one of my pills because I need to be lucid and actually remember this shit even though my stomach is already fucked up for today because of the stress."

Now that he was on the phone, he smiled. He let his working class southern accent seep back into his voice. I watched as he made himself smaller, physically hunching over into his chair, filling his speech with "yes, sirs" and "thank you, sirs."

More than once, he tried to defer to me, but the judge was insistent on hearing from him directly. At the end of the call, after about twenty minutes, the judge assessed that everything seemed in order, and he didn't see any reason why there would be a problem with processing. Then, he raised his voice just a titch; "I hope you know that you are incredibly lucky to have such a kind and considerate daughter. She has managed to save you quite a lot of trouble, it would seem."

I could tell from his tone, and from the way he'd been pressing my father all through the call, that he knew Dad would never understand. He knew what Dad was. He wasn't saying it for Dad. He said it for me.

Thirty-One

After your first Christmas, I was looking
forward to the stillness of winter. Your daddy has
always hated the cold, but I love the chill. I love
the way everything gets quieter, and then the few
sounds that stay - birdsong, leaves rustling,
footsteps - are amplified. I love the way the
horizon turns burnt orange in the evenings and
how the air always smells just a little special
right before the snow.

your first snow

settles.
black trees pale to grey, then white.
crows bob and play, black
and glittering against the quiet sky.
I watch a squirrel skitter up the closest tree,
irritated at the birds in his way.
you miss it all, snoring
delicious and warm.

I would wake up every day feeling a little
less hollow. I would see your daddy reach out to
hug me, and when we connected, I would close
my eyes and breathe him in. I would imagine love
wafting off of his skin like cologne, filling me up

with every breath. I wanted to be close to him, to
curl up inside his heart, but I was also terrified of
getting too close. I was terrified of where it might
lead.

dear husband

I miss you. but
even the idea of kissing
scares me -
suddenly
the idea of
immaculate conception
seems plausible,
and I would rather
set myself aflame.

I was constantly torn between wanting to go
to him, to go back to what we were, and
becoming a permanent celibate. Even though you
were constantly on me, I felt absolutely touch
starved. My body, somehow, understood the
difference between your tiny grasping fingers
and the kind of touch that comes from mutual
want and love. Only, my stupid traumatized brain
wasn't letting my body do what it wanted.
    I was too embarrassed to talk about it with my
shrink, and talking about it with your daddy only
made the hunger worse, and yelling at myself in
the mirror wasn't getting me anywhere. Besides,

I was supposed to be working on being kinder to myself, wasn't I?

So, I did my best to negotiate a truce; I filled up on as many handholds and hugs and lingering forehead kisses as I could stand and tried to believe that, one day, my brain would start trusting my body again.

In the meantime, I tried to lean into my relationship with you. A relationship with you: it was something that seemed a little more appealing every day. I found myself watching you, not out of obligation or fear, but because your toenail, or the way your hair caught the sunlight, stirred something up in me that was warm and soft. I found myself wondering if your eyes would stay this impossible blue or if they'd turn chestnut like mine.

"I think his eyes look like mine," I told your daddy. "What do you think?"

Your daddy came over to investigate. "Yeah. They *are* more almond, like yours, aren't they? Everyone always says he looks like me, but I don't really see it. I mean, he's pale like me, but just look at those cheeks. Those cheeks are all you."

For the first time in my life, I felt something other than disdain over my ridiculous baby fat cheeks. I didn't feel disgust, or disappointment either. I felt that same soft warm something stretching out into the corners of my chest and smiled. The feeling lingered, like I'd been wrapped in the most delicious blanket, for the rest of the afternoon. Late that night, as I was curling up with you to sleep, I noticed the faintest trace of something spectacular coming from your head. Ever since we'd brought you home, every other mother who'd met you would take a deep whiff of your head and smile; "oh yeah, that's the stuff," they'd say. But you always just smelled like a baby to me. Nothing special.

But that night? That night I understood.

skin to skin

> I lean into your
> skin and breathe a sweet
> mushroomy
> milky
> magic. the warmth of you
> floats up to me -
> you are light wrapped in skin,
> curled sweet in my arms -
> the perfection of it
> chokes.

I wanted to hold on to that feeling, that smell, just as tightly as I found myself wanting to hold on to you. Then, a few days later, my reproductive system forced the feeling from my fingers. Or, at least, that's how it felt.

I'd had one short period earlier in the fall, but it had only been notable in that it was my first after having you. Unlike my periods before pregnancy, it had been short and light and hardly there at all. But now? In the dead of winter, my body was furious with me. I imagined it screaming at me, raging that I had refused it the chance to get pregnant again; *how dare you deny me what is rightfully mine!*

loss

great red clods -
mounds of sodden dirt -
I feel each one
like a dropped
egg.
as they flush
goodbye, I wonder:
in another universe,
who would they
have been?

The pain was triggering in a way I was unprepared for. Each cramp, a small contraction, sent my body into hypervigilance. I knew I was not pregnant. I knew I was not in labor. But it felt like I was. I hurt in the same places. My breath caught the same way. I doubled over, clutching at my scar, as I flashed back to your birth. It didn't matter if I closed or opened my eyes; I saw the maternity suite, the chair they'd sat me in, the nurses who held me down. The whole apartment suddenly smelled like rubbing alcohol and cleansers.

it's dark in here again

I don't want to die.
I just want to turn off for a while.
still, I tell your daddy: "hide the knives."
I might
change my mind.

I tried to remember what I'd told myself after
your Daddy had gotten back from his trip; I
swam my way out before, I could find my way
again. But, I didn't believe it, not really. And, over
the course of the next eight days, when I did
manage to stop sobbing long enough to believe I
would find myself again, the idea of drowning
every single month until menopause was enough
to send me screaming. I would, throughout each
day, hold you and search my body for that
sweetness and warmth I'd felt just days before. It
was gone. My chest was, somehow
simultaneously, filled with an icy water and
howling wind.
On the ninth day, I woke up calm. I could tell I
wasn't bleeding any longer, and I was amazed at
how even keeled I felt as a result. I watched you,
still mostly asleep as you reached out towards
the dust that was lit up by the sunshine. For just
a flash, the word *mine* echoed in my head. Your
daddy watched us warily, and I smiled at him.
The way the tension fell from his eyes nearly

broke my heart. None of this was fair to him, either.

"I think I should go see the obgyn," I offered. "I don't think that was normal."

"Probably a good idea," he agreed. His phone pinged and he looked down, reading an email. "Looks like they found a contract for me," he said with a wide smile. "I'll start at the new company next month and we can finally move."

"So, we're moving?" I was trying to wrap my head around it. "We just got here."

"It sure seems that way, doesn't it," he said. "God it's going to be a bitch to box everything up again. But," he paused and came over to us. He put his arm around me. "This is what we wanted, right? Now I won't have to travel and we won't have to live with two big ass dogs in an apartment anymore."

"No, it's good," I said. A strange sort of sadness washed over me. "It's been a good little place though." I reached out to touch the nearest wall. "She kept us safe here in this little cocoon."

eight months

is all it took for this apartment -
with its broken stove, and missing drywall,
and drafty windows,
to finally feel
like salt and incense, dog and you.
I will even miss the sirens.

Thirty-Two

The first time I ever felt aligned with Spring
was when I was pregnant with you. It was
impossible not to. By February, I was six months
along. There you were, growing and hibernating
inside me, preparing yourself to blossom just like
the few brave crocuses poking out of the
still-frozen ground. It gave me such purpose,
knowing you were there. From the very
beginning, your existence has pushed me to do
better, be braver, try harder. I knew what it was
to have a mother who was terrified of her own
shadow. I knew what it was to have a mother
who made herself small. I wanted more for you.

run

I will tell you:
RUN.
I will whisper it
into your life (*run*)
headfast and fullspeed
towards
the wonders
the terrors
the wilds
of this quickly dying world.
be afraid (it's ok.

we all are, little boy)
but
don't let that stop you.
you deserve the light that comes from
careening through darkness. So,
close your eyes if you must, but
run.

All winter, I had been trying to grow with you. I was on forums every day, looking for strategies to better handle Dad. I talked to my shrink about wins and frustrations, and I leaned more on your daddy, forcing Dad to interact even more with him instead of me. I started writing letters to you, begging you to love yourself no matter what and reminding you that there is nothing more precious than the kindness waiting inside you - your gift to yourself and the world.

(Looking back, I don't think those letters were as much for you as they were for me - my subconscious cheering me on - and, a few months back, I burned them knowing neither of us would need to be reminded like that anymore.)

With every letter, my words grew stronger on the page. I found the smallest bits of confidence building up inside of me. I was hopeful, too. Dad had been on a vitamin D therapy long enough now that, when we had his levels rechecked, he was back within a safe range. That meant, I hoped, that his mood swings would begin to subside. *Sure, he's a narcissist,* I thought. *But he was really sick. Now that he's getting healthy, he'll stop. He'll go back to trying to love me again. He'll put his mask back on.*

Then, his primary care doctor suggested a hip replacement. This time, the specialist was warm and inviting, happy to offer a clear solution: between the arthritis and muscle atrophy from the last year, his office was surprised we'd waited so long. Unlike the issues with his throat and stomach, this was a straightforward and fast procedure. We were able to schedule things almost immediately. Then, within just a few weeks, the surgery was done.

Of course, he was still in quite a bit of pain shortly thereafter, but the physical therapy person was optimistic, and Dad had started talking about getting outside again. *He was just in pain. See? He'll stop now. He'll love me again.*

Still, I couldn't help but notice that for all his talk of going for a run around the neighborhood in the very near future, he wasn't following the physical therapist's instructions; he wasn't doing his exercises, and he was still spending most of his day in his chair.

Whenever I'd remind him of this, he'd tell me that he wanted me to do them with him or that he was just too unwell. I refused to exercise with him, though, because I knew he'd just spend the time talking about how fat I was, or how I should be really concerned that I had to modify things for my ever-swollen joints. Instead, I would pivot:

"Do you want me to talk to the therapist for you? Are the exercises too hard?" Irritated, he'd shut down. "No. I'm just tired. Leave me alone."

So, I did. I reminded myself that he was seeing a physical therapist twice a week and an exercise coach once a week; it was really okay to let them worry about it. But, as the weeks went by, and his pain increased as a result of his actions, he took even less care with his words around me. He got into the habit of suddenly needing things in the middle of the night.

After a few days of waddling up two sets of stairs only to find out he wanted to complain about something he'd seen on television, or that he wanted to tell me about his latest decision to change his diet - yet again - I decided it was time to stop going up once the sun went down. Instead, I sent your daddy. Even if I was awake, your daddy would say I was sleeping, and take care of whatever it was instead. Soon enough, Dad stopped unless there was a legitimate emergency.

Then, I took another step. Instead of allowing him to monopolize my entire day, I whittled one on one time with Dad down to maybe two hours, and during that time I stayed busy with crafting or writing or texting friends. Happily, if I really focused on my task, Dad sort of faded away. Occasionally, he'd break through with a comment or criticism, but I would put my hand over my stomach and refuse to react with anything other than a placid smile. Still, I couldn't help but notice he wasn't bothering to couch his criticism of me in backhanded compliments anymore; instead of throwing passive aggression my way for a few hours, he was getting quicker to outright insults.

I figured it was like what happens with a dog, or a toddler; they ramp up once a boundary has been imposed, so they can see if you're serious or not. Even when the new routine is to their benefit, they fight. Like when you punctured my eardrum from screaming over the loss of your bottle. You hated it, but you needed it. If I just stuck to my plan, I thought, then he'd learn I was serious; he wasn't going to be allowed to shit all over my life anymore, and he was going to have to take care of himself. *I just need to give him space to test the fences.*

I was such an idiot.

Early that March, I needed to drive him out to the city for a follow up with the cardiologist. After his heart attack back in the fall, the ER doc had mentioned he might need surgery. Last time, this doctor had seemed uncertain, so he wanted to get another look at Dad. Only, the last time we'd gone, Dad had complained about the stop and start of highway driving. So, as a treat for him, I researched how to get there via backroads. "It only takes ten or so extra minutes," I told him the day before. As an unexpected surprise for me, he'd seemed pleased.

The day we left, though, he was visibly unsettled. I thought, perhaps, he was anxious. I mean, he hardly left his room anymore and now we were traveling a good hour away. I understood. It was easy to empathize; Grandma had experienced the same issue towards the end of her life.

Additionally, while I felt confident in my ability to get us there, I had quite the driving phobia back in my late teens, and anytime I have to drive in heavy, city traffic (as I would that day, since the hospital was in the middle of the city), I still get a little unnerved.

It had to be done, though. He had to go, and I had to drive him. So, I reminded him to take his pills, made sure I had cash for the parking valet, and double-checked the directions one last time.

Situational agoraphobia aside, Dad normally loves being in the car. My dad has always loved driving, or being driven, anywhere. He's a huge car nut. So, I turned the radio on to a station I knew he would like, rolled the windows down to his request, and got going, almost excited for a peaceful hour on the road. I knew once we were out, he'd settle into it like he always did.

"Where the hell are you taking me?" he asked. It had been about fifteen minutes.

"To the cardiologist," I said. I was suddenly concerned he didn't remember and that's why he'd been acting all odd.

"I know that. I'm not an idiot. But where the fuck are we?"

"Oh." I was relieved. "We're just taking the back way. You said you wanted to try to stay off the highway. It's actually prettier than I thought it would be given the time of year."

We came to a stoplight. From my phone, the navigator offered up the next set of directions.

"It's unbelievable how much you rely on that stupid thing," he spat at me. "I mean, how the fuck at you going to manage driving around with a kid in the backseat if you are having to listen to this stupid thing every damn minute. You should know where the fuck you are going."

My hands gripped around the wheel as I tried to understand why he was mad at me. "I do know where we are going," I offered. "But this will tell me if there's traffic, or if there's an accident, so we don't get stuck anywhere. I don't want us to get lost. "

I didn't understand. Using a GPS system had been a key tool in overcoming my driving phobia. He knew that. Hell, he had encouraged it. He bought me my first dashboard system, back before they came preinstalled on phones. He knew I still had to fight back panic attacks if I ended up taking a wrong turn or had to be rerouted for construction and didn't already have the system running.

I cannot tell you how many times he had praised me for finding this way to cope with my attacks, for using technology to my advantage. It was one of the few things about him that was consistently not shitty. But now?

For some reason, that was all suddenly invalid. He was picking a fight for no reason, and I didn't understand it at all.

"You are over thirty years old. You should know how to fucking drive. And roll my fucking window up. It's the middle of goddamn winter."

I did as asked. For a moment, I contemplated pulling the car over. I thought about it; *once the light turns green, I will pull through and then pull over. I will get out of the car and I will start walking, in any direction, and call my husband to get me.* But, I couldn't do it. I was frozen in that car seat with my hands curled around the wheel.

I didn't cry, but I didn't numb out, either. I remember being surprised by that and while I wondered why I wasn't dissociating, I hyper-focused on my hands. I focused on my fingers, one at a time, watching how the skin stretched as my grip tightened with each pulse of panic that ran through me.

The light went green, and I drove. I kept thinking about what he had said; "driving around with a kid in the back." In a year, that would be true. In a year, there would be a baby in the back when I drove Dad to his doctor's appointments. In a year, there would be a baby in the back when Dad told me I should "know how to fucking drive."

In a year, there would be a baby in the house, listening when Dad told me I was selfish, listening when Dad complained about my cooking, listening when Dad told me I was fat like that was a bad thing, listening when Dad implied I wasn't smart enough to take care of the house and hold down a job.

Listening, listening, listening.

And he'd learn... the little boy inside me would learn to hate me, too.

No. NO. NO!

I thought it so loudly I'm surprised I did not somehow smash the windows of the car.

No.

My father would not fuck with my baby.

No.

I don't know how, I thought to you, rubbing my belly ever so discreetly, *but we are leaving. After you are born, I am done.*

We pulled the car into the valet, and I turned on my customer service auto-smile. Surrounded by people, I felt a bit safer, a bit more able to breathe. Dad tried to strike up a conversation, but I ignored him and went to get our parking ticket.

In the elevator, he smiled at me. "I'm sorry if I came off kind of harsh," he said. "I just want what's best for you and the baby. I know how hard it is, you know?"

I nodded. "Of course," I said. Then, I went silent.

"I mean, having a kid is really difficult," he continued. "You need to know what you need to know."

I nodded again and left a small smile on my lips. We got off the elevator and into the waiting room. We were alone, and he continued to try to justify his behavior. I pulled out my notes about his medications and symptoms. When he paused, I looked up; "I really want to focus on this," I told him. "I don't want to forget anything and have to come back."

It was so weird to see him off balance. I'd be lying if I said it wasn't thrilling to suddenly have that sort of power. I watched as he considered his options while we waited. We were moved from the waiting room to the exam room, and he tried to start up again. "I don't see why you're being so difficult about this. I'm trying to tell you why I was doing what I was doing - since you obviously didn't understand -"

I cut him off. "No," I said. I kept my voice light and polite, as if I was dealing with a rude customer in a retail store. "I understand. But I don't want to talk about this now. I want to make sure I have all my notes in order, and I want to be able to focus on what the doctor has to say. I certainly don't want to come back here next week. Do you?"

He shook his head and turned to stare outside the window.

The appointment itself was quick. The doctor asked a few questions, took a few notations, and decided that surgery would be the best thing. It wasn't an emergency, he emphasized. He wanted to wait at least another month for Dad's hip to totally heal. But, he told us, it was a better safe than sorry sort of situation. I took my notes and contemplated how the hell I was going to manage Dad after heart surgery when I was eight months pregnant. It wasn't going to be pretty. That much, I knew.

On the drive home, Dad was tentative. He asked me to reiterate what the doctor had said, and I did. A few minutes later, he asked, "why are you being so combative?"

"I'm not." I kept my voice chipper. "I'm just trying to focus on driving. Isn't that what you wanted?"

"No," he clarified. "In the office. I was trying to talk to you and you kept ignoring me. Do you have any idea how that feels? To be trying to say something important and have the other person just... ignore what you are trying to say? It really sucks," he said, raising his voice a hair. He raised his voice again. "I mean, I was just trying to explain why I said what I said earlier and you wouldn't even listen!"

I took a breath and felt panic rise up along with his voice. I felt you flutter inside me. *It's okay,* I thought. *We're okay. We're just going to get home and get to your daddy and everything will be okay.* "That must have been really frustrating for you," I offered. But I refused to do what he wanted. I refused to ask him to say what he wanted to say. I refused to give him an opening to yell at me some more. He mumbled something, then turned to glare out the window.

"Did you want to listen to any music on the way home?" I asked.

"No."

"You're right." I said, forcing a smile. "I'm sure I'll concentrate on my driving much better in the quiet anyway."

Thirty-Three

Sometimes, in my dreams, Dad and I are walking through the neighborhood and talking about the future. Occasionally, you are with me. Most often, though, it's just the two of us. We pass a row of townhomes and he mentions that we should probably start looking for a bigger place now that you are here.

"Actually," I say, "I think it's time Tim and I tried living on our own for a while."

"Oh?"

"I love you. And I have loved a lot of things about living with you. But, I think it's time."

He never really seems to completely understand what I'm saying, but he smiles at me and gives me a half hug with a kiss on the forehead. "This one is so pretty," he notes. He gestures at one of the townhouses and the door drifts open, inviting us in. "Why don't we see if you like it." He lets me go in first, and we spend the time talking about what furniture I'd put where and he finds a sweet little corner to stick a rocking chair for when he comes to visit.

But, I never got to have that conversation, and he will never come to visit.

***

When we got home from the cardiologist that day, I continued to refuse Dad the opportunity to gaslight me. Over the next few days, I was pleasant with him, and I brought him food, but every time he tried to bring it up, I changed the subject. I would sit with him through a television show or two, but the moment he tried to go back to that day in the car, I made an excuse to leave.

Eventually, he switched tactics and bought me a pair of sunglasses. If you are unfamiliar, this is commonly referred to as love bombing. I was insulted at the obviousness of the move, and I was furious at the idea that he thought the only thing he needed to do to get me to ignore his abusive behavior was spend thirty dollars on a pair of sunglasses that weren't even my style.

Even after that day, the idea of leaving was still enough to send me dry heaving, but Dad did me a favor in a way. All of this attempted gaslighting and lovebombing and just straight up shitty behavior solidified the decision in my mind. We would stay until you were born and I was healed from the birth. Then, by the time you were six months old, we would leave.

"You know," your daddy said, "there's a chance this will kill your relationship. Right? I mean, he might not take it so well."

I knew he was right, but I refused to accept it. I refused to even consider it a possibility. "I think we just have to lie," I told him. "If I say 'I'm leaving because I can't stand to be around you more than a few hours at a time because you are toxic and bad for my mental health,' I'm pretty sure we're burning a bridge. But Dad has always been about the bootstrap narrative. I think if we can sell that we want to go out on our own to show him," I rubbed my stomach to indicate I was talking about you, "that it's important to stand on your own two feet, then Dad might just accept that."

"But we're already on our own two feet. We help pay for everything."

I chuckled darkly. "Yeah. That's true. But that is absolutely not how Dad sees it."

I texted Josh. "Need your help with something. Can we get together for lunch this week?"

"Everything okay?" he texted back.

"It will be," I replied. I wasn't sure I meant it.

I'm not sure I'd have ever characterized my relationship with Josh as close, but, unlike Will, he was still willing to be my brother. We got together for lunch from time to time, chatted regularly on the phone, and did our best to stay connected. He's always been kind of a shit, but in a sweet, endearing sort of way. The running joke has always been that Josh isn't the kind of guy to help you carry your groceries into the house - even if you ask him - but he'll come get you out of a burning building. Given that it felt like my world was on fire, it seemed like it was time to fill him in.

A few days later we sat down with him. I knew he'd never believe me if I just told him we wanted to live on our own without any additional explanation; for years now, I'd gone on about how wonderful it would be to live with Dad when we had our kids.

So, I had to come clean about what was actually happening in my house. To be fair, I'd never lied to him. I'd done my best to be honest with him about how Dad was acting as a patient and how he treated me, but I also spent a lot of time downplaying it. I'd say things like, "Dad was really short tempered today, and he said some pretty shitty things, but I know it's just because he doesn't feel well. I'm fine." Now, I was having to walk all of that back.

He asked a lot of questions, but he seemed to believe me. When I told him about what had happened in the car just a few days ago, his face fell. "I mean, I always knew he was kind of an asshole, but really?" He turned to your daddy, who was nodding sadly.

He apologized for not seeing the signs sooner, and for anything he'd done to make me feel like I couldn't be honest with him. "I gotta ask," he said. "Is this like Mom? Do you even want a relationship with him after all this? Because if you need to cut him out, I get it. But, like, I'm gonna need a bit of time to get him set up with a nurse and whatever else he needs."

"No," I told him. "I just want a different kind of relationship is all. I'm even happy to still help out. I'll bring him groceries, or I can take him to doctor appointments. I... I don't want to lose anyone else. I just can't keep things going this way. It wouldn't be fair to him." I looked down at my enormous stomach.

He nodded. "I get that," he said. "And I get that you don't want to tell him yet. Besides, I bet just knowing this is going to happen is going to take a hell of a lot of stress off of you. We can take time before you leave, and you can show me some of the records and stuff, so I can help out more with him once the baby comes."

The joy I felt at being taken seriously, at knowing he had my back, at knowing your daddy and I weren't alone in this fight anymore – it was overwhelming. Even after all these years, he still didn't totally understand why I couldn't have a relationship with Mom and would still, from time to time, act as if he didn't believe me about her and my stepdad. But *this*? *This* he understood. Thank God.

I struggled to speak, and I fought against tears. Hesitantly, I asked if, in the meantime, he would be willing to drive Dad to at least some of his appointments given what had just happened. "Totally," he said. "Just give me enough notice to request off work, and I'll make it happen."

We spent the rest of the time talking about logistics. Together, the three of us decided it would be easiest to leave when you were four months old. That way, we could be out and settled by the holidays, and, if Dad decided he wanted to sell the townhouse, we wouldn't be doing it in the dead of winter. In the meantime, we'd start packing our things and keeping them in the utility room. When I asked when he thought we should talk to Dad about it, my brother took his time to think.

"I think he'll believe you more if you wait until the baby is born," he said. "If he doesn't understand, I can just blame it on your new-mom hormones; you know, remind him nothing major is changing and you two are still good."

I could feel the knot of stress and fear coiled up around my heart start to unwind. My brother could do no wrong in my father's eyes; if he was on my side, Dad would eventually come around. That's how it had always been. My limbs went weak as the stress flooded through and out of my system, and your daddy helped as we all went outside.

In the parking lot, I hugged Josh as tightly as my belly would let me. "Thank you," I whispered, "thank you so much for understanding."

"Of course," he said. He pulled back and offered me an easy smile. "Anytime."

He gave me one last squeeze then got into his car. Your daddy and I leaned against one another and waved as he drove off.

"It's going to be okay," I said. The words felt so weird in my mouth. "It's really going to be okay."

Thirty-Four

I still don't entirely know what happened. I have talked about it with friends. I have processed it with my shrink. I've journaled and meditated and rehashed it over so many times with your daddy that I've lost count. I suppose though, the truth of it is that I can tell you *what* happened; I just have no damned idea why.

Two days after we met with my brother, your daddy and I got up on a lazy Saturday. Dad was asleep. We took care of the dogs, then decided to drive over to our favorite coffee shop. It was a wonderful breakfast. I'd been having trouble eating lately, but that morning I was famished.

We shared biscotti and bearclaws while we talked about moving; did we want to stay in the area? Did we want to move closer to friends? Did we want to do something crazy and leave the state? How would the dogs handle it, we wondered. I took a minute to consider each possibility, envisioning you running along different yards in different houses. You always looked so happy.

After we ate, we did what we normally did when Dad was still asleep on a weekend morning; we stopped at a fast food joint and grabbed a few breakfast sandwiches. While we were in the driveway, I got a text from Dad. "Don't forget the coffee," he teased.

I chuckled at the joke. Dad hadn't had coffee in years at this point; it made him violently ill. Still, sometimes he'd ask for it the way a little kid might coyly ask for a unicorn or pony, or the way I'd occasionally lust after a designer leather coat or ridiculously overpriced piece of furniture. I knew I was never going to have it, but talking about it was still fun in a self-deprecating sort of way.

"Looks like he's in a good mood this morning," I noted. "I guess he actually slept."

When we got home, we said hello to the dogs and then took Dad's breakfast up together. We walked through the door, both of us smiling. Dad, however, was not. "Took you long enough," he spat.

I struggled to adjust to his apparent mood change. I had not been expecting this version of him. "Oh," I stuttered. "I'm sorry. Everything is here, though. Nice and warm."

"Great. You two have a nice leisurely morning and just leave me here for hours to starve." He grabbed the bag from my hand. I noticed your daddy move closer to me. He reached into the table next to Dad, looking for the stash of paper plates we kept there. He handed one to Dad. His expression was as confused as mine.

Dad rummaged through the bag aggressively. I guess he was making sure we ordered what he had wanted. Once he'd counted the sandwiches, he looked up at me. Something in his eyes was different than I'd ever seen before. He was menacing. "Where is the coffee?"

I smiled. *Oh. He's just putting on a show. He's fucking with me.* I waited for him to smile back now that I was in on the joke, but his expression never changed. "Well," I said, voice shaking, confused, "We thought you were joking. We didn't think you were serious. I mean, you never -"

"Well then you'd better go fucking get it," he growled. He leaned forward in his chair, and I had to fight the urge to step back.

"There's no reason to talk to her like that," your daddy said, calm. "We didn't realize."

"Oh this is all just a fucking joke to you, huh?" He took the bag of food and hurled it across the room. Then, he slammed the drawer full of plates so hard that it popped back open, sending the table into an uncertain wobble. "I am a grown ass man, little girl, and if I want a cup of fucking coffee I will have a cup of fucking coffee."

"Okay," I mumbled. "Sure. I mean, I guess we can."

Your daddy spoke over me. I remember his body language was that of a man trying to reason with a drunk. But I wasn't able to process what he said.

"I will talk to my goddamn daughter any way I goddamn please," Dad bellowed back. He grabbed the shelf to my right and pulled himself to standing. The shelf swayed towards me with it, and a few items fell over onto the floor. As he stood up, Dad forced himself forward and into my space. I had to hop back to keep from getting knocked down.

"I don't understand." I whispered. I wasn't outwardly crying, but I could feel the sobbing inside my skull. "I don't understand." From my peripheral vision, I could see your daddy still trying to reason with mine. Dad slammed the drawer again, and I watched in horror as the wood along the drawer's face cracked. That had been Grandma's. *Is he going to hit me?* He took another step forward, rocking the shelf. I got hit in the shoulder with a few books as I scurried back.

"Fuck you both," he roared. "Get the fuck out. Just go."

I looked up at him. I searched his face for something - I don't know what, exactly. I didn't find it, whatever it was. He was a tower of rage. Inside me, you fluttered up and under my ribs.

"Okay," I whispered. Then, stronger. "Okay. Fine. We will fucking go."

After we left the room, I stood on the stairs for a moment, trying to breathe, while your daddy ran around the house to fill backpacks with our most-needed things. I heard Dad sit back into his chair.

"Sweetie?"

He called my name gently. For a moment, my heart leapt. He was going to apologize. He was going to tell me he needed a hospital; he'd had some sort of event. He hadn't meant any of it.

"Did you want me to come back in?" I asked, trying to match his tone.

"No." His voice went flat. "I just wanted to say I think you're being a real bitch."

By the time I made it downstairs, I'd completely dissociated. From somewhere above, I watched myself gather a few items of clothing, my favorite stuffed animal, our medications, and the book with all our important documents. Your daddy grabbed the dogs, and then we were racing across the parking lot with Dad hurling obscenities at us from his open window.

I don't think I said anything for the first twenty minutes. It took me that long to realize we were moving. "Where are we going," I asked. I watched the dogs in the rearview window as they enjoyed the breeze from the drive.

"I called Logan," he said. "We'll stay with him while we figure this out."

"You mean while we find a place to live."

"Yeah," he reached out to hold my hand.

"Because we can't go back there," my voice was airy. I felt like I was hearing someone else say the words. Her voice solidified and turned serious. "We can't go back there," she said again.

"No, baby." He said, softly. "We can't."

"I don't want to leave everything behind again," I whispered. I flashed back to being fifteen years old and filling my backpack with everything it could carry while I waited for Dad to come get me from Mom's. In my mind's eye, I watched my younger self, torn between wanting to stay and needing to leave. "Why..." I sobbed hard, choking on the words. "Why am I having to do this all over again?"

"It'll be okay," you said. A prayer and a mantra. "It'll be okay."

Thirty-Five

When you were nine months old, we moved one state over to a new home. In a lot of ways, it was less stressful than the last time we'd moved; after all, this time, it had been our choice and on our timeline and for a wonderful reason. Still, I struggled as I put our belongings back into boxes and packed up the apartment. I'd just started to feel safe. What would happen to me - to us - when we moved somewhere new?

Additionally, you were outside of me now: a living squirming thing to keep track of. The one benefit to moving at eight months pregnant had been my nesting instinct; I'd unboxed and decorated like I was in some sort of trance back then. Now, the idea of making a new house into a home while you were crawling under my feet seemed unfathomable.

It was all terrifying, but it was wonderful, too. In those quiet moments when you were asleep or bouncing in your walker while I did dishes, I'd daydream about life after the move. The new place had a little yard you could play in, and a little deck we could laugh on, and there were playgrounds everywhere in the neighborhood. I thought about walking you up to the library, or taking you to the local farmer's market. I hadn't seen the house in person, but your daddy had

265

shown me pictures. It was an even nicer place than what we'd left behind with Dad.

"I think you'll be really happy there," I'd tell you. "The neighborhood is supposed to have lots of other kids to play with. Won't that be nice?"

You'd babble at me while I packed away our clothes and told you all about the different things we'd see and do. "We can get you swimming lessons," I said. "You love wiggling around in the bath. I bet you'd get a big kick out of a pool. I wonder if your daddy would want to take you." I reached over to tickle your toes as they danced in the air from the middle of the bed. "He loves to splash around almost as much as you do."

Unfortunately, during the chaos of packing, my period came again. And, just like last time, it shoved my head under the water and held me firm.

'there's screaming inside my head."

the words tumble out.
I am dying
of embarrassment, shame. overwhelmed
at how crazy I sound.
"Tell it to shut up,"
you say.
but I can't.
so you say it. over
and over, until all I hear is you and our son,
who is laughing.
until all I hear is
my son.

When I was done bleeding, I found myself again. It was like a lightswitch turning on and off. Crazy. Not crazy. Depressed. Not depressed. Suicidal. Peachy-keen. It was ridiculous in a horrific sort of way. I made an emergency appointment with an obgyn at my practice. At the time, there was some kind of disease spreading; no one knew what it was, exactly, or how it spread. I hated the idea of catching something from the doctor's office, but I could not go on this way.

She perused my file while I talked at her, trying to express the gravity of the situation, frustrated with myself for not following through with a doctor the last time this had happened and scared she'd see that as proof I was overreacting now.

"Here's the thing," she said. "It's actually pretty common for women with ppd to develop pmdd. That sounds like what might be happening here." I was stunned at the matter-of-fact way in which she spoke.

"So," I struggled to stay calm, "you're telling me it's normal that I hallucinate and want to kill myself and don't really care what happens to my son for a few days every month? Really?"

She raised an eyebrow. "You didn't say anything about hallucinations or suicide. Are you at risk?"

I laughed at her. "Currently? No."

"And your child?" Now she watched me carefully. Her eyes met mine. "Is he at any risk?"

"No," I said, irritated. "And it would be nice to have your full fucking attention because you are worried about me. The mother. Not just my goddamn child."

"Again," she said, patient. "You did not mention hallucinations or suicidal ideation."

"I'm sorry. I said 'seeing things again' and 'want to do bad things.' My bad. Given that those things are in my chart from multiple doctors, I'd just assumed you'd connect the dots."

She sighed like I was being a bitch. I guess I sort of was.

"Why aren't you on birth control?" She asked.

"Because the thought of my husband touching me gives me a panic attack," I replied. "And I had an IUD, but it fell out."

At this, she smiled. "Birth control is often a very effective treatment for pmdd," she offered. "What were you on before the baby?"

In the end, we settled on a low dose generic and she told me I'd be feeling better within a week. "Certainly your next cycle will not be as bad," she assured me. "And they should get progressively better over time."

For the first couple days, they did seem to be working. It was like someone opened up the curtains inside my brain. I felt almost manically joyful. I took advantage of the energy and packed up boxes with gusto. I took you and the dogs on long walks and came home with enough energy to cook dinner.

no such thing as bad weather

It's raining - fat,
warm splats of water
crash down as if someone tipped
a bucket over upstairs. you lift from my chest,
and stare into the sky.
your face struggles for the right emotion, and
then
you're laughing - Laughing!
It comes just as fast and loud as the rain and
now we're laughing together and the dogs are
in the background, pissed off that we are
standing still but I...
I would stand in this moment forever.

I felt alive. Lit up. On fire. "Maybe this really
will help," I told your daddy. "Maybe this was all I
needed. Just some really good drugs," I teased. I
hugged him in a way I'd forgotten was possible.
Then I kissed him in a way I thought I'd never be
able to again. My body gave way to his like a
house happy its inhabitants were finally back
home. "I missed you," I whispered into him. "I
missed you so much." He kissed at my tears, then
at the rest of me.
The following morning, he found me on the
kitchen floor.

untitled #3

I will get a hysterectomy, I tell you.
I will cut it out.
I will not lose myself
I will not lose my son
I will not keep drowning.

With a rusty knife if I have to.
I will make them take it all.

He helped me call the doctor's office to let
them know I'd had a bad reaction to the
medication. I confirmed that I was at the wrong
part of my cycle for these symptoms, and they
made note. They told me it would take 24 - 48
hours for the medication to get out of my system.
I did my best to hold my breath and wait.

she reminds me I'm not alone

"Everything is muffled,"
I tell my shrink.
Like I'm covered in gauze
or at the
bottom

of a well. I tell
her I don't want to be numb,
but the alternative
is killer.

As promised, the meds did leave my system. I could tell because I wanted to hold you more and more. I noticed the pink in your cheeks instead of the black in your eyes, and I heard your babble like music instead of screams. You were coming back to me, and I was shocked at how much joy it brought me.

"I don't want to stop liking him," I told your daddy. "I... I have these moments where I almost think I might one day maybe love him, and they feel so right and soft and perfect, and they keep getting washed away, and I have to start all over again. I don't want to keep doing this," I told him, burying my face in his neck. "What if this is how I am for the rest of his life? What if every month - forever - I have a few days where I hate him? Where I keep having to remember how to be his mom..."

The thought broke me. I curled around him and sobbed. "My parents hated me. They hated me and I know it. I always knew it, and I – I can't do that to him. Please don't let me do that to him. Please."

" Baby," he whispered. "Look at how upset you are. Do you think either of your parents ever worried this much about you?"

I sniffed and pushed the snot aside with my shirt sleeve. "Yeah, okay," I admitted. "You might have a point."

"We'll move, and we'll find you a new doctor, and we will get this sorted out. We will find a way. Okay? I promise."

We said it together: "it will be okay."

Thirty-Six

Your daddy had known Logan for years, but I'd only met him a handful of times. I'd never met his wife. As we hurried into their beautiful house, they both worked hard to make me feel comfortable. Their three kids bounced back and forth, watching our dogs play with theirs, and everyone kept asking me questions about when the baby would be coming. Everything about it hurt: the laughter, the light streaming through the windows, the tasteful kitchen, the friendly smiles.

Everything was a reminder of the life I thought I was going to have. The life I killed any hope of having just an hour and a half ago. Sure, Dad was the one who lost his mind. But I was the one who left. I knew enough to know that it was permanent; there was no salvaging my relationship with Dad now. I may as well have killed him, and I grieved accordingly.

Logan's wife made sure I got something to eat and drink while I told her that I wished we'd met under different circumstances and she, the lovely host, deflected gracefully. Then, when I could hardly stand any longer, I waddled down the steps to their basement spare bedroom.

It reminded me of my room at Mom's, tucked away from the rest of the house. As I headed down, they apologized for the fact that it tended

272

to hold on to the chill from the cement utility
floor and cinder block walls, but I thought it felt
amazing.

It got colder with every step down and, for the
first time in months, I wasn't overheated. By
myself for the first time, I sank into the bed and
looked around, trying to process where I was and
how I'd gotten there. Above me, I heard the dogs
careening back and forth and their girls laughing
along. It was a wonderful sort of noise. The sort
of noise I'd always hoped for.

"I'm homeless," I said aloud to no one. I was
trying out the words. Trying to figure out how to
explain them to the few friends I had. Trying to
figure out how to get myself to push the buttons
on my phone to call them all. They were going to
ask so many questions, and I didn't have any
answers. You were due in less than two months.
Where would you even be born?

"I'm homeless," I said again.

"Only a little," your daddy teased. I didn't see
him walk into the room, but there he was, sitting
on the bed beside me. I smiled at his joke. He was
used to couch surfing; he'd spent a good portion
of his teens and twenties existing on the kind will
of others. I knew he'd know what to do. I tried to
hold on to that knowledge as I struggled to find
the energy to use the phone.

"Logan says we can stay here as long as we
need to," he offered, gently. "But you don't need
to worry about that. I will find us a place. A place
for us and the dogs. We'll be safe." He got off the
bed and squatted down on the floor to look up

and into my eyes. "We will be okay," he said firmly.

I nodded. Then, I took a breath and picked up the phone. It was time.

After forty-five minutes, three different calls and a handful of text threads, I was exhausted.

"I am so proud of you," one said. "You did the hard thing for you and your baby, and I am just so fucking proud of you."

"We can lend you money for movers," another said. "So you can get it all at once."

"I've got a storage unit," another texted. "And we can come help you get your things."

"I love you. You two take care of us all the time. It's time for payback, okay?"

"You are so loved."

"We fucking love you, sweetie. We got you. Food. Clothes. Baby shit. Whatever."

"Just remember," one texted. "You are safe now. Whatever happens, you are safe. We're all going to keep you that way."

It was more love than I could have ever imagined. I had no idea someone other than your daddy could be kind to me like that. After all, I'd never told any of them about what I was going through. Not even my very closest friends. But... they believed me without question. Even the few I'd considered more your daddy's friends than mine; they believed me, and they wanted to help me. Without question.

I sat, holding that thought in my mind. When was the last time I'd said something to Dad or my brother and had them just believe me? I found myself replaying my conversation with Josh from just a few days ago. How many questions did I have to answer before my own brother bought into what was going on?

For the first time since Dad's outburst, I felt a seed of anger blossom in my chest. It unfurled, pushing my spine straight and forcing my eyes forward. I turned to your daddy and said what I was thinking aloud. I needed to hear it. "I am eight months pregnant," I said. "I am allowed to want to live in a place where I don't get yelled at every day and I'm not scared for the safety of my baby."

"Yes. You are," he said, quiet.

"Do you think I should call Josh now?" I asked. "This isn't exactly what we had discussed. I mean, I know he'll understand and everything. I just don't want him to think we're hiding it. I just... I'm so tired."

"Why don't you call him after dinner? That way you've got a chance to get some food and recover a little before you two talk."

I nodded. Then, as often happens when I am thinking about him, Josh called me instead. The moment I saw the number, I tensed back up. Josh was a creature of habit and process; I knew he'd understand after I'd explained, but the minute he found out that I had deviated from the plan - assuming he didn't already know - he would launch into a lecture. I was going to have to choose my words carefully, bury the lead, and hope Dad hadn't already reached out.

"Hey," I said, letting my exhaustion seep into my voice. "I was just talking about you."

"What the hell," he said. He was furious. "I keep getting these crazy calls from Dad. You just left? Are you insane?"

I shot your daddy a glance to let him know it wasn't going to go well. He squeezed my hand as I took a breath and started to explain. "Did he tell you what he did? He was physically threatening. He screamed at me. He told me to get the fuck out. Repeatedly."

"So you just left?"

"You would rather I stay and get hit?" I spat it out at him. "What exactly would you have done?"

"You take care of everything for him," he said, frustrated. "You can't just leave. He has surgery next week. What do you expect me to do?"

I could not believe what I was hearing. He didn't understand at all. I had a dozen people ready to take up arms for me and my own brother was on the verge of begging me to go back. Clearly, I wasn't explaining it right. I took another breath. "I don't expect you to do anything," I said, calmly. "Just because I will not be taking care of him anymore does not mean you have to start. The man has enough money to hire as much help as he needs now that he's not paying all those credit cards."

"So you are not taking care of him anymore. To be clear."

"No."

"I mean, I guess you have to do what you have to do, but I think it's pretty shitty you couldn't find a way to wait it out. We just talked about this. Are you sure you're not just overreacting like you did with Mom and running away because you don't want to deal?"

My cheeks flushed with rage. *I don't want to lose him too. But I fucking will.* "I'm sorry you are disappointed," I said calmly. "But this is out of my hands now."

"What do you mean? You are the one who left. You wouldn't even stay to talk about it. And now you're just expecting me, to what? I'm not going to take him his meals or drive him to his appointments or any of that. I have a life. I can't just drop everything because you can't handle him anymore."

"I cannot go where I am not safe," I said. I kept my voice cool.

"Well I don't know what you expect me to do."

"You could say you are glad I am okay," I offered. "Or you could say you're sorry things with Dad went the way that they did. Because you know this isn't what I wanted."

"Isn't it, though?" He was cold, dismissive. "I mean, you wanted to leave."

"No," I said, sighing. "I understand why you're upset," I said. I had a sick feeling that this was the end. I thought about all the reading I'd done about narcissists and about their family structure. I'd accepted, long ago, that I was the scapegoat. Now, I was forced to realize another truth: Josh was the golden child, and my actions were threatening everything his relationship with Dad was built on.

I struggled to keep my voice calm. My life with Josh - the most powerful moments of our childhood - flashed before my eyes. I used to tell people that we'd been forged in the same fire; nothing could keep us apart for too long. But now I understood it differently; we may have lived in the same house, but we'd had different parents, different traumas, different worlds. All these years, we'd never known one another at all. I wanted to cry and scream and sob at him until he had to pull the receiver away from his ear, but I knew now. It wouldn't matter.

It wouldn't matter if I cried over how unfair his fear was. It wouldn't matter if I screamed over how he'd never be treated the way I had been even if Dad were dying. It wouldn't matter if I hurled obscenities long enough for him to realize that we could *both walk away*.

We may have been forged in the same fire, but I was made a shield and he a sword. I couldn't let him slice at me any more. *Goodbye.* I said it over and over again in my head, hoping that, somehow, his soul would hear mine.

Goodbye. I love you. Goodbye.

"I know this isn't what we talked about," I said it as gently as I knew how, "but I had no choice. I know that is a lot to process, and I hope you will come to understand."

"You sound like a robot. I'm talking about Dad's life, here. You're just walking out of it and I – I'm not doing it. I have a life. I just don't understand why you couldn't wait!"

Goodbye. I love you. Goodbye.

I closed my eyes tight, forcing away tears. "I am sorry this is difficult for you," I said. I dug my hands into the comforter, trying to hold on. "I understand you are scared. But I did not do this at you. I will put together a binder for Dad with everything I've been taking care of. If you decide to help him with anything, you can hire him a nurse and a maid. He shouldn't need anything else."

"If. Like I have a choice. Fine. Great. That seems like the least you could do."

Goodbye. I love you. Goodbye.

"I know you and I had a running joke," I said. "You take care of Mom, and I'll take care of Dad. And I wanted to hold up my end of that. I didn't want anything that is happening right now. But I wasn't safe there. *My baby* wasn't safe there. I hope, one day, maybe you can understand that."

He paused. "So you aren't even going to take Dad to his surgery next month then. Are you. You're going to need me to do that."

"I love you, little brother. But no. I'll send you a digital copy of the binder in a couple days."

"Great. You do that. That'll fix everything."

Goodbye. I love you. Goodbye.

Then he hung up.

Your daddy rushed over to me as I stared at the now-off phone. I could feel the tears at the back of my eyes and the sobs at the back of my throat, but I couldn't let go of either. That would make it real.

"You did so good," he whispered. "I am so proud of you. I am so proud of you. You took your time, and you told him the truth, and I am so proud of you."

"He didn't listen," I said flatly. "Sure, he's always been an asshole. But, when we talked last week I really thought he understood. I really thought... he didn't, though. I think... Why doesn't any of my family actually love me?" I didn't give a chance to respond. "He's too scared Dad's going to try to turn him into what he turned me into, all broken and sad and small. Why is it okay for me to be that way if it's not okay for him?"

"You don't look broken to me," he whispered. He kissed me hard on the cheek.

"But I am," I said. Then, I started crying. I wasn't sure I'd ever be able to stop again.

Thirty-Seven

We moved with you from our apartment to the townhouse just as the first round of Covid lockdowns went into place. It was a weird sort of blessing; I did want to take you places, but I didn't feel ready for it yet. As much as the idea of carting you around a grocery store or new park made me smile, it also sent me hyperventilating. There were so many things that could go wrong. But now? Now the entire world was screaming at me not to take you anywhere, and I was only too happy to listen.

covid

Around us, the world
is on fire. I try to commit each day
to memory - If we survive,
you will ask
    where we were, and
    did we know, and
    did we know anyone
who died…
for now,
we are here. on a
small slice of clay-coaked earth, surrounded
by seedlings and wind.

You were crawling now, and while you figured out how to gain traction on the new wooden floors, I bleached every possible surface and started to unbox our things. Your daddy was working from home for the foreseeable future now, and he would take frequent breaks to help me move laundry or to let the dogs outside, where they'd do zoomies and chase each other in the frigid January sun.

I spent a lot of time dissociating. I simply could not believe I lived in this space. I could not wrap my head around the idea that I had actively stepped into my new life, away from Dad and the rest of my family. The apartment has always felt like a safe space, but not a permanent one. It was a shelter, but not a home. But now? This was a home. This was our home. It felt like I was in a waking dream.

The only place I felt whole was on the deck. I'd carry you out, with the dogs at my feet, and we'd stare out into the pine trees that separated us from the neighbors across the way. The sun would peek from behind rooftops, and it was quiet enough to hear the mourning doves cooing nearby and the breeze whispering through the trees. I'd nearly forgotten how nature could sound after a year of city living. I'd hold you tight and let you reach your fat little hand out just far enough to touch the closest pine. Your fingers would dance against the needles, and you'd laugh as they poked into your skin.

After a few days, my body was restless for walking. So, slowly, we started exploring the neighborhood. At first, I was worried about running into other people, but it was too cold; no one else seemed willing to go out into the gray. We'd come back inside, pink-cheeked and exhausted, and then curl up onto the couch together to nap. In the afternoons, you'd explore a pile of laundry or a stack of empty cereal boxes while I unpacked. Then, in the evening, I'd cook dinner. It was hilariously 1970's housewife of me, and I loved it; I craved the simplicity and routine.

I don't know how it happened, exactly, but after a month or so, things got easier. Maybe it was because you were getting older, so things didn't seem as frantic; you fought less over diaper changes, you had fewer reflux issues, and you could actually wait long enough for me to make you a bottle if I showed you that's what I was doing.

You were fiercely independent, too. You didn't have much interest in being entertained; you'd sit on the kitchen floor while I did dishes and, occasionally, pull at my leg to show me whatever you'd found to play with. Then, after I'd smiled at you and commented on your amazing find, you'd go off into your own little world again. I'd even started baking bread again; I'd set you in your high chair with your breakfast and we'd dance to the radio or listen to podcasts while I worked. Around us, the world was struggling (and I certainly don't want to minimize the trauma so many have endured), but the lockdowns forced me to embrace the peace of our new home. I didn't have any other choice.

Everything felt slower. Languid. Some days, I'd find myself sitting on the floor with you for twenty minutes only to have my heart go racing when I was sure I'd forgotten something. Only, I hadn't. I tried to remind myself that I'd spent the better part of a decade taking care of two elderly family members, maintaining our house, and working 50 hour weeks. Compared to all I'd been doing before, taking care of one small infant and keeping the house tidy was really easy from a labor management perspective; it was going to take some time to adjust.

Once a week, my therapist would check in digitally. Because of the lockdown rules, she was still able to see me virtually even though we'd changed states. I remember I was filling her in on all my progress around the house and my plans for the backyard. "I want him to know I'm the kind of Mom who wants him to explore," I told her. Then, I stopped. I replayed in my head what I'd just said. "Huh. When did that happen?"

"What?" She asked.

"Normally," I explained, "when I go to say I'm his mom I have to, like, take a big breath before and sort of minimize it after and do all this internal ridiculousness to remind myself it's okay to be a mom that doesn't always like her kid and doesn't even know if she loves her kid and just now I didn't do any of that. I just... referred to myself like I was his mom. Because, you know, I am."

"How does that make you feel?"

I am
a Mom.

Holy

fucking
fuck.

That's not to say I was all better, though. For a reason I couldn't quite understand, I was not able to sleep with you upstairs in your bedroom. Every time I tried, I would start to shake and need to scream. So, we continued to co-sleep on the couch. On top of that, I was still plunged back into a suicidal depression every single month. The only difference was that the time between the episodes was better each month, a little easier each month, and I liked you just a little bit more. My heart would walk right up to loving you, then my period would hit and any potential love would disappear.

It'd be a Wednesday, and I'd find myself kissing at your toes or snuggling along your cheeks with the same sort of warmth I felt for the dogs. Then, I'd wake up that Thursday and feel nothing. I'd stare at you and feel... nothing. It would be nothing but a sobbing abyss inside my chest for days. Then, five or six days later, I'd hold you and feel a spark again.

amen

I finally stop bleeding -
for the first time in days,
I think I might love you.
    (please, universe.
    please
let me keep this
    feeling...
    I need this child
to know love.)

I'd made an appointment to see someone back
when we had moved, but it had taken until now,
in late March, for me to actually be seen. I went in
my mask and watched the women in the waiting
room. I wondered morbidly what it was like to be
pregnant during a plague. Then, half an hour
later, I got to tell my story all over again.

"Normally we prescribe birth control," she
suggested.

"It makes me want to kill myself, so what else
have you got."

"You're already on an SSRI, right?"

I nodded. She shifted in her seat,
uncomfortable. I knew why; I'd just shot down
the most common two treatments for pmdd and
my face made it very apparent I wasn't going to
leave empty handed. I took a breath.

"Here's the deal," I said. "I will go as off the
wall or whackadoo as you want. You heard of a
supplement that's not FDA approved? Sign me

up. You want me to shove a crystal up my hoohah and do a little chant under a full moon? Great. You want me to try a little known surgical procedure or new medication? Awesome. Because I swear to God if I don't get this under control I am legitimately going to request you take the whole thing out and just take the side effects that come with early menopause. I. Cannnot. Live. This. Way."

She leaned forward in her chair and set her laptop down on the table beside her. I watched her look at me - really look at me - for the first time since she walked in.

"Are you taking anything at all now?" she asked.

"I'm scared to take the wrong thing," I told her. "I've just been focusing on my weight. I'm down a little over 70 lbs, which means I've almost lost as much as I gained with him, and I keep expecting that to make a difference - and it does, to my joints and my pelvic floor issues - but not for this. I still go crazy."

She nodded. "Okay." she said. "There's some evidence that fish oil can help, and it would be a good idea to start taking magnesium to help get better quality sleep. You can take vitamin B - the liquid one - and vitamin D is always a good idea. And get yourself a good multivitamin."

"Anything else?"

"Just... try to remember it can take up to two years for your body to figure itself out after pregnancy. Sometimes three. So, it's going to be a

process. I'm not saying we can't get it better. I
think we can. But it's going to take some time."
   I nodded. "I just... I just need a step in the
right direction."

   After a couple weeks, I noticed a difference. I
still wasn't sleeping much what with you waking
every two hours for the bottle, but when I did
sleep, I wasn't waking up with muscle cramps or
spasms. I wasn't hitting my afternoon slump as
hard, either. I was still tired, but I wasn't
sit-in-a-corner-and-cry exhausted. My squats and
walks felt just a smidge easier. I started to let
myself imagine a life where I wasn't depressed a
quarter of the time and terrified of that quarter
for the rest of it. I started to laugh again, and
mean it.

   we are

   three humans, two dogs,
   and thirty five plants
   between us.
   we are sticky, and covered
   in fur, and living
   dangerously on high
   fructose corn syrup
   and caffeine.
   it is delicious.

The real test, though, came two weeks later with my next period. I could tell it was coming because my hip joints got loose and my tailbone was trying to fall out again. Then, the day before I started bleeding, I woke up in the Bad Place. But, I was only there for a day. As an added cause for cautious optimism, within a few hours of actively bleeding, I felt emotionally stable.Sure, it still felt like my insides were getting ground up into hamburger, and every single joint in my body felt structurally unsound, but I wasn't lost. I wasn't crying. I wasn't missing the part of me that loved holding you.

sweetness

the sky is painful blue,
but, somehow, I
breathe it in.
I am holding you, the dogs
are playing at my feet and yes. Yes...
I remember this -
this
is happy

I spent most of my time at Logan's sitting in the sun. The rest of the world might have felt chilly during those early March days, but you were a furnace inside me. I was content to waddle, barefoot in the dew-covered grass, wearing a pair of pajama pants and an enormous men's t–shirt your daddy had bought for me from the thrift store. We still didn't have any of our things; not that my clothes would have really fit anyway.

While I sat, I'd watch the dogs explore their new home. His backyard was almost an acre; they'd never had land like this. Even from the depths of my depression, I loved watching them chase after one another and dig after smells. They were their most dog selves, if that makes sense, and it seemed like the one good and immediate thing to come out of the horror show I was living in.

march

the sky
is the kind
of blue I thought
only existed in technicolor

movies - ones with cotton
candy songs
and problems easily
solved by supper

    It didn't take long to put the binder together for my brother, but emailing it over to him hurt. It was another nail in the coffin: another act of mine that was ensuring our relationship was dead. Your daddy would constantly remind me that I didn't start, or do, anything wrong in all of this. And, he was right. But it didn't matter. Grief is grief no matter who causes the loss.

    For the entire time we were there, every single day, something small or funny would happen, and I'd want to text or call Josh about it. He'd always got a kick out of hearing about the dogs' antics, and he thought my pregnancy was fascinating in a scientific sort of way. I'd pull out my phone to send him a picture or tell him about a lung-kick from you, only to remember: he didn't want to hear from me like that anymore. We weren't those kinds of siblings now.

    Looking back, I'd swear it was longer, but we only stayed with Logan and his family for a week. During that time, your daddy found an apartment for us that was dog-friendly and in a not completely shitty part of town. Then, he worked with a hostile Josh, along with a whole crew of our friends, to coordinate getting a moving truck down to our former home.

At first, I wanted to go with him, but someone needed to stay with the dogs; more importantly, I wasn't sure I could handle watching my friends actively dismantle my things. It took my breath away just to think about it; if I had to watch them take my art off the walls or box up my afghans, I might disintegrate.

After a very long day, your daddy came to get me and the dogs, and I saw the apartment for the first time. It was a cute little two bedroom ground floor unit with a bright kitchen and huge windows. There was a tub big enough to fit my ever growing belly, and the whole place felt like it was reaching out to me: *you are safe here, little one.*

While your daddy leashed the dogs up for a much-needed walk, I set about unpacking my plants; our friends had boxed them gingerly, so I could take my time pulling each one out. I checked their leaves, watered their soils, and gently arranged them around the space. "There," I whispered to them. "You're home."

Over the next few days, I set to work unboxing and organizing. At this point in my pregnancy, I ached from stem to stern, but I still had absolutely no problem moving boxes of books around the room or lifting shelves to clean the carpet underneath. Your daddy would leave for the office in the morning, and I would start. Around noon, I'd collapse and get the dogs for a short walk, and then I'd start again. After a week, I'd managed to make us a home. There was only one problem; we were missing a bunch of stuff.

Even after renting a moving truck and enlisting five friends to help, your daddy still hadn't been able to get everything. They just hadn't had the time. We tried, repeatedly, to coordinate with my brother to find another day to go down, but he refused to commit to a time. It was always, "we'll figure it out," or "I need to check my work schedule," or "don't worry. We're not going to toss it." Which, of course, just made me worry more.

He did try once, though, to reach me, specifically. He texted your daddy's phone and asked to speak to me; he texted me that Dad was willing to go to family therapy if I would go home.

"That's not my home anymore," I texted.

"Fine. Whatever. Then go to keep a relationship at all," he texted back.

I considered it. I knew it was stupid; I knew Dad would just lie, or love bomb me in front of the therapist. I knew therapy with narcissists never worked. But, maybe that was okay? If it meant I got to keep a relationship with him and my brother and still didn't have to move back in… maybe that was ok? I mean, wasn't that what I wanted at the beginning of all this? When I told your daddy what I was thinking, his face went dark.

"I wasn't going to tell you this," he said. "Because I know what it's going to do to you. But, if you're really thinking about this then you need to know." He paused and, instinctively, I sat down. You swam up under my ribs as my heart raced. "When we were there, I saw our neighbor, Sara."

"Oh?"

"Yeah" he said, slowly. "And she went out of her way to tell me how happy she was that we had taken the dogs with us."

I waited.

"Twice, she nearly called animal control on him because she saw him yelling at and hitting the dogs. It was loud enough for her to hear from the other side of the parking lot."

I stopped breathing.

It all made sense now. Why the older dog would never be left alone in his room with him, and why the younger dog was constantly pissing in corners of the house. Why they both got so upset when we left to go anywhere, and why the younger dog howled if you went anywhere near his ears.

I'd left my babies alone with him, and he'd hurt them.

I'd trusted him, and he'd hurt them.

He. Hurt. Them.

I fought to breathe and wondered if you could literally drown from guilt or shame.

"I... I ... I should have known," I finally eked out. "I knew he blew pot smoke in the baby's face, and I tried to get him to stop. I should have known." My voice got louder as I struggled to get the words out over my wails. "He always hated that they weren't his precious Duke. I should have known."

The dogs came rushing over to me. They licked at my face and hands, and I grabbed one in either arm and pulled them closer; "I'm so sorry. I'm so sorry. I'm so sorry." I said it over and over, breathing in their fur, until we settled into a pile on the bed.

Your daddy watched us silently. When I looked up to him, he looked like he'd been crying. "So, you see why you can't now," he said, soft.

I nodded, resolute. "He will never know our son."

Your daddy nodded back.

Rage started to unfurl in me again, then, too big for my body to handle, it disappeared into a cold resolve. "Our son will know safety. He will know what it is to be safe." Then, I texted my brother. "No. And I want the rest of my things."

A full month went by. While Josh refused to pick a day for us to gather our belongings, he started to pressure me about the house itself. My brother was demanding I sign the deed over to Dad now that I wasn't actively living there anymore.

In theory, I didn't have a problem with this, but I was on the mortgage, too. So, he was asking me to sign away any potential equity while still staying on the hook for the payments. After consulting with a lawyer, I realized what he was asking wasn't even legal, and wondered if Josh was being manipulative or just stupid.

Dad's surgery was still on my calendar, and it was coming up, so we figured the best thing to do would be for your daddy to go to our former house while Dad and my brother were at the hospital. There weren't many things left, anyway: a few paintings, some holiday decorations, and grandma's ashes. He should have been able to fit everything in his car.

Unfortunately, when he went down, he ran into something unexpected: they had changed the locks on us. When your daddy called to tell me, I was beside myself. After all, my name is on the damned thing. I called the police and asked if I was allowed to smash in the window of my own house. The officer on the other end of the line was all too happy to report that yes, I could take a baseball bat to the sliding glass door if I felt so inclined. I just needed to have all my paperwork in order.

The idea of a nearly nine month pregnant woman smashing through a window with a beat up baseball bat was the first thing to bring a smile to my face in days, so I had your daddy pick me up. We grabbed some food, dropped the dogs off at Logan's, and headed back down. I made sure to have all my paperwork with me, just in case.

Surprisingly, though, no baseball bats were required. The front door was unlocked and open. Dad was home from surgery, and my brother was with him. Given that it was heart surgery, I had assumed they'd keep him overnight; the idea that he might be there had never occurred to me. I took a step back from the house, not sure what to do, but your daddy took another step forward.

"They saw me through the screen door," he said. "May as well go in."

I remember my brother and your daddy having a heated conversation, but I couldn't process what it was about. I caught a glimpse of Dad, propped up in a recliner at the other end of the floor, and hurried into the kitchen to avoid his glare. Quietly, I started to box up my spices and the few dishes that were gifts from your grandma.

"Get out here and talk to me," Josh demanded of me. Hands shaking, I set my things down and stepped into the hallway.

"I have a right to my things," I said, quietly. I did my best to sound brave. "Get her ashes," I told your daddy. "The rest isn't important."

Your daddy moved across the room to grab the urn, and my brother stopped him. He grabbed your daddy's hand and slammed his own onto the table, making everything in the room shake. "You're going to want to get off me," your daddy said. He kept his voice calm and low. Josh did, and they both slowly backed away.

Josh turned to me and screamed. "Don't you see that I don't want to deal with this? I spent all day at the fucking hospital taking care of *our* father and you - you come here and don't you get it? I don't care what is going on with you. I don't care. I don't want to deal with this. Me. ME."

He walked towards me as he spoke, and his voice continued to rise. It was the second time I wondered whether or not someone I loved was about to beat the shit out of me.

"Then I'm calling the cops," I said, and I left. We waited outside for half an hour or so. When the cop arrived, we showed him the proof that I co-owned the building, but all he did was ask my brother politely to allow us in. Obviously, Josh refused.

"You can file a petition," he explained. "And I'm sure it will be granted. But I can't allow you to just walk in and take what you want."

I still don't fully understand why he couldn't, but I wasn't about to get arrested over it. Then, I realized I'd left my wallet and phone in the box in the kitchen, and he was kind enough to retrieve them for me. Shortly after, his car drove off, and we followed suit.

We were quiet for most of the drive home. "I promised Grandma," I whispered. "She wanted me to spread her ashes over the bay, and I promised her right before she died that I would. And I never told either of them because they didn't love her and they didn't care and I know they wouldn't anyway. And now they are just keeping them to fucking spite me and I can't do like I promised."

I felt apart, crying into my open window.

"You know damned well that she wouldn't care," he said. "I mean, it would have been nice, but would she want you to be this upset over this?"

I sniffed and chuckled. "No. She'd actually be really pissed at me," I admitted.

"Okay," he said. He squeezed my hand. "Let's go get our idiot dogs and head home."

It was the last time I ever saw either of them.

Thirty-Nine

A little over a year later, we were finally settling into our new home. It was April, and the entire world seemed to be sprouting up in celebration of the coming spring. Great purple waves of wisteria clung to the trees, and the smell filled the air for miles.

With everyone still in lockdown, or working from home, I got into an easy routine of texting and calling friends; we were farther away from everyone, but I felt closer than ever. For the first time since having you, I felt something other than lonely. And, for the first time, I felt a kind of safety I had never known before. It was unsettling, in a strange way, to be so devoid of fear.

Sometimes, we would all go out to a nearby meadow or a few steps into the woods, and I would be gripped with a sense of peace and joy so overwhelming that I numbed out before I had the chance to stop myself. Or, I'd dissociate and see myself from above and hardly recognize this relaxed person leaning against a tree in the afternoon sun.

under the trees

I watch you dance with your daddy

- eyes shining, face pink, hands
reaching out
in delight - he laughs as if
he's always known you.

I spent a lot of time talking to my therapist
about it, and she reminded me that our brains
are creatures of habit. "Even if what you're used
to is terrible," she said, "your brain is going to
crave what it knows. So give it time. It takes time
to learn a new way to live."

A new way to live.

Her words stuck with me, and I mulled them
over constantly.

What kind of life was I going to have now?
Who was I going to be? For better or worse, I'd
always considered panic attacks a cornerstone of
my personality; I was the well meaning but
socially anxious one in the group. Now I was
starting to wonder... I was going whole days
without them. And the space between them was
growing wider all the time. Was I going to stop
having them one day? If I wasn't the girl who had
panic attacks, who was I?

Another, smaller thought was growing louder,
too. Was I even a girl at all?

I was starting to think maybe not.

I wasn't ready for that, though. Not yet.
Instead, I pushed the idea of gender aside and
focused on the one that came before it: if I wasn't
the girl who had panic attacks, who was I?

I tried to imagine what I would tell you if you came to me asking for help on how to find your way back to yourself. I decided I would probably tell you to start with what you absolutely knew you loved. So, that's what I did.

My first project was to turn our back yard into something more than a pine-needle and dog poop rain pit. We were doing better financially, but hardly had extra money lying around for landscaping; so, I strapped you into your carrier, and we wandered into the woods for river rocks, pebbles, and baby ferns. I'd fill a backpack, then carry it all back to the backyard and carefully arrange our finds.

You weren't overly interested in the woods, but you loved to play in the yard. At first, you hated the feeling of your bare feet on the earth. You were fascinated by the bits of shining mica in the soil, though, and you thought the few blades of glass were hilarious when they brushed against your skin. Dad had used to yell at me all the time about walking barefoot, but now I could do so in peace; the soft soil warmed in the sun, and I taught you to dig your toes all the way in.

Beyond the garden, I let myself fall back in love with kitchen work again and made bread as fast as we could eat it. Thankfully, you thought the process was hilarious.

kneading bread

the rhythmic
dough on counter
draws you close.
you swim across the floor,
tug at my feet, and
babble. while I rinse my hands,
a familiar song
comes on, and you
wiggle
with dancing. I sing along,
loudly, and laugh
at how gentle
our life has become.

I still struggled, though. You'd started teething, and the precious little sleep I was getting was compromised further. Your daddy and I even went back to shift sleeping for a while, but it wasn't enough. Even though we were weeks away from my period, I was shifting in and out of the Bad Place.

search party

on dark days,
(when I cough
up the water that's
at my neck)
I search for her

(for you). I scream into the waves,
looking for your mom
and pray
you can't tell that I've
lost her.

At the same time, you were starting to
boundary test in earnest, and it was triggering as
hell.

promise

You slap me. It's harder
than I expect, and
something in
the sting rings familiar.
I am reminded: one day soon, you will be
a man.
In the remembering,
I am terrified
of you.
I force myself calm, and curl
your fingers around my thumb.
We stroke my cheek.
"Gentle," I whisper. A promise and a prayer.
"Always gentle."

Still, I was excited to see you evolving into
more of a person and less of a potato, and I was
amazed at how your growth affected mine. I

remember trying to explain it to a friend; "he's a totally different person every two months," I said, "he is capable of completely different things, wants brand new things, and interacts with the world in a completely new way. And that means… that means that, as his mom, I am constantly changing. Who I was as a mother, what he needed from a mother even just four months ago is different than what he needs now."

They nodded as if they understood. I continued. "It makes me wonder about other parts of myself," I mused aloud. "Like, who will I be in another three months? Will I be the kind of person who, I dunno, whittles? Or takes up tap dancing? Will I be nonbinary? Or more?"

I stopped. I tried to make it seem like I was naturally taking a breath before moving on, but the truth was that I'd said the quiet part out loud. I hadn't even talked to your daddy about my gender identity. Yet, here I was, trying it on.

When our friend left, I brought it up to him.

"It's not that I think I'm a guy," I said, slowly and full of anxiety. "I just don't really think I'm a girl, either."

As usual, he was obnoxiously unsurprised.

When I talked to my therapist about it later that week, I told her I was worried to own this new particular truth. "I don't know if I'm running from something or to something," I said. "All my life, the people who have hurt me the most have painted me in the most feminine of ways. Right? So, am I running from being femme because I don't want to be hurt anymore? Or am I running towards masculinity because that's what I actually am?"

"Does it matter?" She asked in that exasperating way that therapists do.

"I guess... I guess I've always been masc of center," I considered. "Sure I went through a poppy princess phase in my twenties, but who hasn't? But even then... I never really felt like I spoke "girl." It wasn't like I was wearing clothes. It was more like I got to wear these wild costumes. Like every day was Halloween and I was going as a "girl.""

For a few minutes, we sat there staring at one another on our screens. *How many times*, I wondered, *am I going to realize something about myself that feels like it's changing the very earth on which I stand? This shit is exhausting.*

Then, I perked up. "Ooh. This means I can get a new name!"

"True," she said, "but your current name is often used for guys, too. Isn't it?"

"It is," I said. "But every time I hear my name, I hear echoes of Dad hissing it at me or Josh groaning it at me or Mom spitting it back in my face."

She nodded, and I continued. "My name means brave," I said. "I think I lived up to that pretty well all these years. But I don't want to be brave anymore. Rather, I don't want to have to be." For a moment, I heard my deadname in my family's mouths again. Then, I shook my head and refocused. "I'd take my Grandma's middle name for mine even if it is femme as hell, but she hated it and would probably haunt me out of spite."

She laughed and I brainstormed some more options.

Later that week, I sent a text to my friends:

Plot Twist! Turns out I'm nonbinary and my name is Skadi. Hi!
Everyone was delighted for me.

You, however, were going through a hell of a time. You were desperate to drop your only nap. I have no idea why. Napping is amazing, and the entire pediatric medical establishment was pretty vocal about the fact that you still needed two. Still, no matter how much I begged, you refused to yield. You would be exhausted (we both would be), eyes rimmed with dark circles your head heavy on my shoulder, keeping yourself awake with the sheer force of your screams. You were as stubborn as your mommy and daddy combined.

I would hold you tight against my chest while I whispered into your ear:

you are safe here

I recognize the panic
in your screams - they ebb and swell
with the pain
of not knowing...
where do I go, mama, when I close my eyes?

I don't know, little soul.
not really.

A week or so later, I decided to try a different
tactic. A friend of mine suggested I start offering
you quiet time: a chance to play independently
somewhere safe while I laid down. It felt wrong,
and it took some time for you to stop screaming
at the baby gate like a wrongfully imprisoned
Lifetime Movie actor, but, before long, you were
quietly destroying your playroom while I hid on
the floor behind the couch. I couldn't sleep - I
was always worried you'd need me and I
wouldn't wake up - but I rested.

I'd read some trashy news, or I'd watch a short
show on my phone, or I'd just close my eyes and
breathe. And, even though you weren't sleeping,
the lull in your day seemed to soothe you as well;
I'd release you after an hour or so, and you'd
emerge relaxed and smiling. As a bonus, you
would end up so exhausted at the end of the day
that we started to be able to put you down
earlier and you were falling asleep faster than
you had before.

I was still sleeping with you, so I would go up
to bed with you even if the sun was still up and I
wasn't quite able to fall asleep myself. But I didn't
mind; there was something luxurious about lying
in bed at seven thirty with you snoring beside
me. I'd catch up on the news, or do a little
writing. Then, come late April, I found myself
logging onto dating sites again.

I wouldn't start dating again until well after your second birthday, but it felt wonderful to feel like I could consider that part of my life again. Even though I kept it clear on my profile that I wasn't looking to actually meet up with anyone anytime soon, I went ahead and changed both my gender identifier and my name. The rightness of it kept me smiling for days.

Then, that May, you had three teeth cut through all at once. I didn't even need to use the thermometer to tell you had a fever. Your face was the wrong kind of flushed, and your eyes had that glassy, faraway look. Not long before this, I would have been terrified. But that afternoon, your fragility didn't scare me. It didn't hurt, or intimidate me, to know you were going to be needier that your usual self. When your clammy hands, unsure and unsteady, clawed at my skin, it didn't bother me. All I felt was calm.

"Come on, little bit," I murmured. "Let's help you sleep."

lullabye

we sway in the safety
of Sun.
    Who knows
    how long
    I've loved you
at first, your fever rivals her heat.
    You know
    I love you

> *still*
but she cradles us, wraps us
in the softest swaddle
while I sing.
your body sighs,
falls harder
against mine.
> *Will I wait a lonely lifetime*
your breathing slows.
there's a breeze, birdsong
then snoring.
> *If you want me to, I will*

I don't know how long we stood there in the backyard before we went to curl up on the couch, but I remember that the dogs were asleep on the porch behind us, and the sky was a cloudless blue.

I remember that the river stones were cool under my feet, and that the hum of the HVAC unit behind us whirred up through my toes.

I remember the air smelled like fresh mulch and cut grass, and that the top of your head smelled like honey and sweat.

Mostly, I remember whispering a new truth over and over again: "I love you. I love you. I love you."

Epilogue

It took a full extra year before I managed to find a way to consistently manage my pmdd. Truthfully, even now, when you are almost four, some months are a crapshoot. I've been to new doctors, tried new supplements and protocols, and even braved retrying an IUD. Some days, I still daydream about cutting it all out, but those days are fewer and farther between. More importantly, it's been over a year since I couldn't find my love for you.

We stayed in the townhouse for two years altogether, then moved again. Now, we have space, and there is land, and our first night here a bear walked right up to our trashcans to say hello. Our house is full of color and life and laughter (and sometimes screaming because you are still not quite four). I still have days where sleep deprivation drives me into the Bad Place, but that's what naps and espresso are for.

Shortly after moving, I realized I am transmasc and sent about another round of *Plot Twist* texts. Everyone has been supportive, and I am grateful everyday to be this loved.

Eventually, the fact that I owned property with Dad came back to bite me in the ass. It took almost as long as it took to write this book - two years - to cut that particular tie. There were lawyers, and tears, and a fair amount of

screaming, but, in the end, I was able to walk
away with enough money to pay everyone that
needed paying and my freedom intact.
  I now have nothing tying me to any of my
family of origin except these memories.
  I am free.
  We are free.

lucky

like, when you couldn't dare to be brave
enough to ask for what your whole body
screamed with needing because asking made it
true and the heartbreaking that could follow
would be enough to topple whole civilizations.
  but
  we asked anyway. Didn't we,
  little one?

  and it is beyond.
  beyond anything I had any right to hope for.